From Planned Psychotherapy to Gestalt Therapy

Essays and Lectures — 1945 - 1965
Frederick Salomon Perls, M.D.

Frederick (Fritz) Perls

WITH A FOREWORD BY PETER PHILIPPSON

A Publication of The Gestalt Journal Press

A publication of
The Gestalt Journal Press
P. O. Box 278
Gouldsboro ME 04607-0278
USA

ISBN # 978-0-939266-90-6

From Planned Psychotherapy to Gestalt Therapy

Essays and Lectures — 1945 - 1965
by Frederick Salomon Perls, M.D.

Gestalt Therapy on the World Wide Web

The Gestalt Therapy Page is the Internet's oldest and most comprehensive web resource for information, resources, and publications relating to the theory and practice of Gestalt therapy.

Visitors can subscribe to News and Notes, a free email calendar of conferences, training programs, and other events of interest to the worldwide Gestalt therapy community.

The Gestalt Therapy Page includes an on-line store that offers the most comprehensive collection of books and recordings available – many available nowhere else!

Visit today: www.gestalt.org

The Gestalt Journal Press was founded in 1975 and is currently the leading publisher and distributor of books, journals, and educational recordings relating to the theory and practice of Gestalt therapy. Our list of titles includes new editions of all the classic works by Frederick Perls, Laura Perls, Paul Goodman, Ralph Hefferline, and Jan Christiaan Smuts. Our catalog also includes a wide variety of books by contemporary theoreticians and clinicians including Richard Hycner, Lynne Jacobs, Violet Oaklander, Peter Philippson, Erving & Miriam Polster, Edward W. L. Smith, and Gary Yontef.

In 1976, we began publication of The Gestalt Journal (now the International Gestalt Journal), the first professional periodical devoted exclusively to the theory and practice of Gestalt therapy.

Our collection of video and audio recordings features the works of Frederick (Fritz) and Laura Perls, Violet Oaklander, Erving & Miriam Polster, Janie Rhyne, and James Simkin.

The Gestalt Journal Press, in conjunction with the University of California, Santa Barbara, maintains the world's largest archive of Gestalt therapy related materials including original manuscripts and correspondence, published and unpublished, by Gestalt therapy pioneers Frederick & Laura Perls and Paul Goodman. The archives also include more than six thousand hours of audio and video recordings of presentations, panels and interviews dating to early 1961.

CONTENTS

On Roots and Rootlessness: Drifting, Searching and Flying

INTRODUCTION

Perls trained as a neurologist at major medical institutions and as a Freudian psychoanalyst in Berlin and Vienna, the most important international centers of the discipline in his day. He worked as a training analyst for several years with the official recognition of the International Psychoanalytic Association (IPA) and must be considered an experienced clinician. Behind the popular image of the eccentric from the American West Coast, there is a man who stood as a lifelong representative of the so-called Expressionist generation. (Bocian, 2010: 21)

I am honored to be invited to contribute the Introduction to these papers. They form a vital part of the intellectual history of Gestalt therapy, a history which is, in the main, not taught or understood in much of the Gestalt world — to our detriment. In this Introduction, I want to think around this history to see what is going on, what process leads us to an ignorance of our founder's ideas. For he was Gestalt therapy's major founder, in two ways. First of all, theoretically: while Fritz took ideas from his wife Lore (Laura), who had a strong background in philosophy and Gestalt

From Planned Psychotherapy to Gestalt Therapy

Psychology, and other people he encountered (Smuts, Goldstein, Reich and Sullivan prominent among them), and allowed his ideas to be extended by Paul Goodman, Isadore From and others, it is clear from these papers that the synthesis of these ideas into a framework of a unified therapy was almost entirely that of Fritz Perls. Secondly, it was the skill and excitement of his demonstration work in the early years that enlisted people across America to the cause of Gestalt therapy (in a way that Laura Perls and Paul Goodman did not: Laura Perls mostly remained in New York and Paul Goodman's interests were far wider, extending into political, educational and social concerns).

Fritz Perls the wanderer

> Many Jews could have been saved during the Hitler regime if they could have let go of their possessions, relatives, and fear of the unknown. (Perls, 1992: 127 *unpaginated original*)

My parents, like Fritz and Laura Perls, were refugees from the Nazis. The sudden loss of friends, familiar environment, language, daily routine and the sense of rejection by one's country have a profound effect on a person's life, as well as on one's family. In essence, one has to ride the current using one's creativity and resources to establish a new identity and new supports, or one sinks. In his moves from Germany to South Africa to Holland to America, Fritz Perls lost his nation, his friends, his psychoanalytic training and therapy practice, and his connection to the Bauhaus movement. As the Bocian quote at the start of this piece suggests, the *insider* in a radical and creative German movement, part of a society in turmoil, became the eccentric *outsider* in a conservative America; the well-regarded psychoanalyst (his sponsor to travel to

South Africa was Ernest Jones, the major United States advocate for Freud) became an outsider both to psychoanalysis and to the therapeutic establishment. It is easy to see an isolated refugee from another culture as a figure of fun, and we have been guilty of that form of racism in the Gestalt community. And Fritz Perls made his eccentricity and "letting go" the cornerstone of his later personality. He avoided the familiar and sought the unknown in every situation.

It is moving to read, in "Planned Psychotherapy" in this volume, his response to meeting the people at the William Alanson White Institute, the Institute of Harry Stack Sullivan, Frieda From-Reichmann and Erich From, an institute dedicated to relational psychoanalysis, and finding a welcome. Perls described it like this: "Then a miracle happened to me. A few months ago I met some members of your group, and I was deeply moved as I had been seldom in my life. After all, there were people on this globe who saw the world as I saw it, who spoke a language similar to mine." It was a homecoming experience, yet once again not a home he became fully identified with. He remained the wanderer, with a tenuous connection to wife and family, professional bodies, lovers and places.

But, fortunately for us, Perls was also a wanderer in places of the intellect. He read widely, if not always deeply, but deeply enough to produce a unified pattern that could bring together elements of psychoanalysis, Existentialism, Phenomenology, Kant, Wittgenstein, Gestalt Psychology, Friedländer's "Creative Indifference" (a Western restatement of Taoism by another Berlin Bohemian who attended the same café as Perls), Zen and smatterings of Scientology! And what was the basis of this pattern? It was to bring together unities that had been broken apart by the impact of culture, politics and social anxiety. He was the exile who wanted to make the person-in-the-world whole again, and through this to

From Planned Psychotherapy to Gestalt Therapy

contribute to the healing of the world. In "Psychiatry in a New Key" (in this volume), he writes about the unity of mind and body, and of Conscious and Unconscious; and in "Theory and Technique of Personality Integration" (in this volume) he writes about the "unity of linguistic and structural integration."

Identification and alienation

> These conflicts have one pattern only: the identification-alienation pattern. This means: the patient identifies himself with many of his ideas, emotions and actions, but he says violently "No!" to others. Integration requires identification with all vital functions. Every attempt at integrating is bound to bring to the foreground some kind of resistance, and it is this bit of resistance I am after and not the content of the "unconscious." Every bit of re-sistance that is changed into personality as-sistance is a double gain as it sets free the jailer and the jailed. (Perls, 1948, in this volume)

In view of Perls' experiences, it should come as no surprise that the center of his therapeutic system would be ongoing patterns of identification and alienation, what is joined to and what is discarded. These are central to both *Ego, Hunger and Aggression* (as Perls' symbols "¶" and "‡") and *Gestalt Therapy: Excitement and Growth in the Human Personality* (as the ego functions). The person in Perls' schema continuously forms, assimilates and grows by this orientation, engagement and disengagement. In fact, "self" is itself an identification and "other" is an alienation. In his lecture (in this volume) "Finding Self Through Gestalt Therapy," Perls states his central theme: "The self is that part of the field that is opposed to the otherness." If there were no other, he says, there would be no

From Planned Psychotherapy to Gestalt Therapy

self, just like there would be no day without night to contrast it with. "Self" is a comparison word, and it is always to a self-other differentiation and comparison that we need to look. Self can only be found in its relation to that otherness which I now make figural (a double use of identification and alienation: see Perls on "cathexis" in "Psychiatry in a New Key" in this volume). It was this interest in a relational approach to therapy that linked Perls to Sullivan and the other founders of the William Alanson White Institute.

So the theory of dysfunction that Perls is proposing here and throughout is a splitting-off of areas of relational functioning that seem too dangerous to engage with. This is a truly radical approach. It is not the language of "inner subpersonalities" hidden away defensively in the Unconscious, or bound by Reich's "muscle armoring," but lively, energized "aggressions" on the world turned in difficult circumstances against the self. Rather than being buried "deep," they need continuous interruption and refocusing because they are the person's raw response to their situation, or to unfinished situations pushing for completion, and these interruptions can be observed as resistances. But the resistances are for Perls not problems to be got through, as in classical psychoanalysis, rather a guide to the unfinished relational needs of the client. The aim of Gestalt therapy is to restore the fullness of available contact, so a person can engage in his/her fullest way with what the world gives to them. The therapist is not an observer of the client's process, but an Other in relation to whom the client is Self. The power first seen in the resistance, rather than being "discharged" in a Reichian way, is turned outward to face the world (initially in the person of the therapist). As Perls says in "Finding Self Through Gestalt Therapy" (and in many other places), ". . . the whole catharsis theory is rubbish. Nature is not so wasteful as to create emotions to throw them away."

From Planned Psychotherapy to Gestalt Therapy

On personality

I think the major limitation in Perls' thinking and writing, which was remedied by Paul Goodman's expansion of the self theory in Perls, Hefferline and Goodman, is that there is very little said about the place of assimilated personality functioning in Perls' early writings. Ironically, it seems to me that denying the need for assimilated personality functioning left him with only his fixed defensive personality, the episodically intimate (in therapy and relationships) but overall uncommitted guru. Once again, his process was always to look for the new, and to question the fixed and familiar. And yet it is also in the familiar identifications with friends, family, commitments and values that we can make our lives most complete and satisfying. I can get some sense of how Perls saw such commitments as contributing to the death of friends in Germany who didn't leave before the War, and made a virtue of his flexibility and willingness to throw over all that was familiar. Yet he deprived his children of his commitment and presence, and also deprived the developing Gestalt community of any usable structure for training and certification. After he went to California, he represented what he was part of in New York as now outmoded by what he was currently doing. Thus different parts of the Gestalt world have very different "personalities," depending on the trainers who established institutes, and where and when they got their introduction to Gestalt ideas, practice and ethics.

Finding our roots

It is only comparatively recently that there has been an interest in rediscovering our roots, and critiquing them from a position of knowledge rather than of half-digested fragments. Our founding theory describes self and other co-forming in the process of contacting, and the continuity of self-organization as an achievement (sometimes a worthwhile achievement, sometimes a defensive diminution of our possibilities) rather than a given. Therapy in this understanding is a relational play with self-other possibilities, a challenging of the continuity which prevents the client living fully in their current world and a support for finding new orientation for engagement in the world. There are "parts" to be integrated, but these "parts" are not intrapsychic subpersonalities, but relational possibilities. Emotion is significant in orienting towards contact rather than as an internal event to be fostered or discharged.

Yet we still find Gestaltists who see "bashing cushions" as a method of catharsis (even if Perls saw a method based on catharsis as "rubbish") or Gestalt therapy as a way of adjusting our feelings (as far as I know, Perls never did this. He often got people to exaggerate small movements, and sometimes people ended up hitting or kicking out. But Perls's interest was the awareness and the completion of an unfinished gestalt, never a "discharge"). We still find people who think Perls saw interruptions to contact as pathological and resistances as needing to be destroyed. There are still people who write about "attunement" and "tracking" as if the client shows something objective about their "inner being" of which the therapist is a mere observer. I have come across people who complain about Perls's poor scholarship and yet who could not accurately state his own theoretical position. This is unique in the annals of psychotherapy schools, this ignorance of the founder, and the fact that Perls contributed to this by reinventing his position and discouraging theoretical discussion is really no excuse.

The more I have explored what Perls and Goodman were doing in the 1940s and 1950s, the more I have been able to sharpen my work with clients. I have felt the need to approach some of what he wrote critically, but the overall framework greatly repays the study and helps me know my own roots in a therapy that

From Planned Psychotherapy to Gestalt Therapy

would not have existed if it wasn't for the integrating genius of Dr. Frederick Perls.

So I would commend these formative writings of Fritz Perls to those who would get a fuller sense of the original ideas of Gestalt therapy, a work in progress, but already a fairly consistent field-relational approach to psychology and therapy. My hope is that, with more people reading these papers and our "Bible," Perls, Hefferline and Goodman, the discussion of what is useful and what needs reworking can be grounded in a rediscovery of what is exciting and unique in Perls's ideas.

Peter Philippson
January, 2012

References

Bocian, B. (tr. P. Schmitz) (2010). *Fritz Perls in Berlin 1893-1933: Expressionism - Psychoanalysis - Judaism*. Bergisch Gladbach, Germany: EHP Verlag Andreas Kohlhage

Perls, F. (1992). *In and out the garbage pail*. Gouldsboro ME: The Gestalt Journal Press. Original Publication 1969

From Planned Psychotherapy to Gestalt Therapy

Planned Psychotherapy

Frederick Perls delivered Planned Psychotherapy *at the William Alanson White Institute in late 1947 or early 1948, when the White Institute was New York's primary psychoanalytic training institute and Clara Thompson among its leading faculty members. As you will note, the term "Gestalt therapy" has not yet evolved. This article was published, over thirty years after it was written, in Volume II, Number 2, of* The Gestalt Journal.*

Perls draws connections between his thinking and that of the Gestalt Psychologists, but "Gestalt therapy" is still in gestation.

*　　*　　*　　*

Ladies and gentlemen, every one of you is only too aware that we are born into a time of multiple contradictions.

Up to the 18th century, a spiritual concept of the world, a religious ideology, was, with very few exceptions, taken for granted.

The 19th century saw a break-through of the materialistic approach in science and in the mentality of a great number of individuals. The emotional satisfaction of the religious approach was replaced by the intellectual gratification, by rationalism, predictability and security as far as quantitative calculations could provide.

From Planned Psychotherapy to Gestalt Therapy

Science scored triumph after triumph by its analytical method, by disintegrating the world into particles and arithmetical figures, but a synthesis hardly went beyond the creation of a league of nations and of chemical ersatz preparations.

We suffer, probably more than in any time since the existence of this globe, from doubts and contradictions, from the dualism of mind and body, spirit and matter, theism and materialism. Even the most advanced psychiatric terminology speaks of psychosomatic medicine, as if such things as a soma and a psyche did exist. We have, in general, not yet learned to regard such dualisms as dualities instead of contradictions. No, instead of an integrated mentality, we have an outlook which is a mixture of spiritualism and materialism.

The mechanical age broke with the tradition that the soul is an emanation which entered and left the body with birth and death and at some other rare mystical occasions. Soul and mind now turned into secretions of the brain and ductless glands, and a number of hypotheses, like the association and reflex-arc theory, although contradicting each other, satisfied the mechanically minded. One could cut the brain and the spine into sections and pieces, but one could not integrate them — and one did the same with the so-called psyche.

Three main concepts characterized the mechanistic mentality in regard to psychology, namely:

1. The psyche is identical with consciousness.

2. The mind consists of particles glued together; its functions are dictated by the laws of association.

3. Perception and action are dependent on each other through the neuronic pathways of the reflex arc.

From Planned Psychotherapy to Gestalt Therapy

The incorrectness of the first theory has been proved by Freud, and is today accepted by the majority of scientists.

The second theory is slowly being replaced by Gestalt psychology. Even where the Gestalt theory, as such, is not yet accepted, certain aspects of it, especially the idea that the organism has to be considered as a Unity and is reacting with a Unity of purpose, have found a good reception.

The third theory, however, the theory of the reflex arc, has proved of great value for neurology. No wonder that it is so much ingrained in your pattern of thinking that even a slight doubt of its correctness will arouse in you the same hostility and derision which Freud encountered when he first published his revolutionary ideas.

Tonight I cannot embark upon a discussion of this subject, but I wish only to say that I do not believe that the rays of light, for instance, travel in a mechanical way into the brain and incite there a motoric action. I prefer to follow Professor Kurt Goldstein in the assumption that the sensomotoric system should be considered as two systems, namely, as a sensoric system and a motoric system. I personally would like to add that although closely interwoven, these two systems are the organic aspects of orientation and manipulation. Both orientation — or the sensoric apparatus — and manipulation — or the motoric instrument — have the direction from the organism toward the environment, and not one leading into and the other out of the organism. If you visualize the feelers of an insect, or the baby exploring its primary world by mouth, or the blind man's walking stick or his seeing-eye dog, you get a quick glimpse of the anti-reflex-arc approach. Having thus re-established the sensing into the senses, then philosophy, semantics, theorizing and other means of orientation fall easily into a Unitary concept of the human personality.

The integrative function of the human nervous system finally achieves a specific outlook towards the world, it achieves a *Weltan-*

From Planned Psychotherapy to Gestalt Therapy

schauung. Such a *Weltanschauung* is the map or blueprint for our actions. Thus, as long as the concept of the world is a magic one, psychotherapy is executed with magic rites. We see such a practice, for instance, in Christian Science. A moralistic world concept demands the destruction of Evil. The mechanistic orientation will tackle internal conflicts with bromides, mental confusion with the surgical knife. The purely psychologistic schools will attempt to remove complexes and inconsistencies. The sexual economist will restore the functions of the orgasm.

However, in one respect an understanding of many schools of thought seems to emerge, at least in theory — namely the assumption that the neurotic (and I shall confine myself to him) is a split and dissociated personality and that the cure has to be effected by a reintegration of the personality and its intrapersonal relations.

In spite of this hypothetical agreement, its practical following-up is rather restricted as the continual hostility and bickering — or if we speak in the Freudian jargon, the mutual negative transference — shows.

There are several reasons why only in rare exceptions psychotherapists have reached a satisfactory integration which allows them to spot and to eliminate dissociations within themselves and in others; and there are a number of reasons why such an integration of the individual (and of the psychotherapeutic movement in general) is difficult to achieve.

There are first of all a number of linguistic difficulties. Notwithstanding the fact that language is the basic tool of the psychotherapists it is in many cases taken for granted that either we use the same words for the same meaning as the persons we deal with, or else, we deem it sufficient to define our meaning, expecting that mere definitions can overcome deeply ingrained patterns of thinking.

From Planned Psychotherapy to Gestalt Therapy

If we assume what seems to be the simplest theory — that the modern European and American personality is one which is split into deliberate and spontaneous functions — then we can put down a neurosis as merely being a state of an unsuccessful compromise between these two kinds of functions. Being such a dualistic personality, the modern individual has necessarily also a dualistic mentality and language. He thinks in terms of soma and psyche, of good and bad, of Super-ego and Id, of mind and nature, of Eros and Thanatos, of individual and society. No, we have not yet achieved the tool of a Unitary, of an integrative language. We see dualisms, where there are only dualities or two halves of one-and-the-same-whole, or, in many cases like the human personality, we see objects like the body or the mind or the unconscious where we are dealing merely with different aspects of an organism. We *have* a body instead of *being* one, we have a mind or thoughts instead of being this mind or the thinker. You all know that this disowning of one's properties is especially pronounced in the obsessional character, but it is present in the mentality of all of us, because, after several thousand years of dissociated existence and mentality, we cannot turn the clock back to Heraclitus. We have to forge new linguistic tools adequate to our cultural situation, if we ever can hope to overcome the dissociation of the homo sapiens, if we ever can hope to regain his survival value.

Next to the linguistic, we find a philosophical difficulty, namely the discrepancy between different concepts of integration. Sometimes it is the character which is to be integrated, sometimes the intra-personal relations, sometimes the instincts, and, in most cases, the unconscious and the conscious mind. Often a combination of several aspects is aimed at, but rarely a really comprehensive integration is viewed and planned.

The third point to be mentioned is the sociological question: can we interrupt the vicious circle in which the man of culture finds

From Planned Psychotherapy to Gestalt Therapy

himself? Can a really integrated personality function in a dissociated society? If we pronounce adjustment to the environment as the aim of psychotherapy and stress the importance of security, can we not expect that the Unitary personality will, as a strange phenomenon, encounter hostility and lose the security which a conformistic attitude would give him? I do not think that we can as yet decide this question. However, the mushroom-like growth of interest in psychiatry at present to be found in the U.S.A., shows the spread of neurosis consciousness and the collective insight that something is wrong in the state of Denmark. Unitary concepts are increasing, and, once people in leading positions, as did General Chisholm, realize that the survival value of mankind is at stake, the vicious circle may be broken. In the meantime we can do nothing other than produce Unitary personalities who are willing to live dangerously and insecurely, but with sincerity and spontaneity.

From what I said before, I hope it has become clear that the unconscious or conscious planning of any treatment is dictated by the *weltanschauung* of the therapist. Perhaps one can classify two groups, one which interferes with the biological figure background formation, the other which facilitates it. The first one reduces awareness and self-expression, the other promotes it; the one favors deliberateness, the other spontaneity. A man complaining of sexual impotency went to Coue . . . this example is typical of the whole of the first group mentioned. It is in no way different from the method of the physician who prescribes barbiturates for insomnia. The physician does not realize that insomnia is an attempt of the organism to deal with unfinished problems, unexpressed emotions, or other unresolved situations. He prevents the problem in question from coming to the foreground by prescribing sleeping drugs, which are a very potent means of diminishing awareness, and he thus perpetuates a situation which the organism in its infinite wisdom is trying to resolve.

From Planned Psychotherapy to Gestalt Therapy

The second group — the one to which you and I belong, will favor the natural f/b formation. For those of you who are conditioned to thinking in terms of an organism made up from a number of particles, like associations, the Gestalt psychological approach may provide a number of difficulties. I should therefore explain in brief the relation of the f/b formation to the systems of orientation and manipulation, to dissociation and psychotherapy.

Let me start with my favorite example. A soldier, on patrol in the desert, after days of struggling and marching under the burning sun, returns to camp. His first word is: "water," or, if he has enough strength left he will, oblivious of anything else, approach the well. An hour later, he will be astonished to find his best friend offended for not having been congratulated on his promotion. Yet our friend had bragged to our soldier about it immediately upon his return.

Our soldier has, during his desert march, lost a certain amount of water — the physiologist would say he is dehydrated — his organismic balance is disturbed, until he has regained a sufficient amount of this fluid. His sensoric tool provides him with a twofold orientation, with an internal — namely the sensation of thirst and the emotion of longing — and with an external one. The world around him becomes irrelevant except for anything related to his thirst. Only a brook or a bottle of beer or something similar jumps into existence, that is: evokes his interest, becomes the figure, the rest a dim background. His friend's enthusiastic remark did not exist for him, he actually heard it as little as you receive the sounds of a clock of which you were aware, before becoming absorbed in a book. He had receded so much into the background that it did not exist for him. On arrival, our soldier manipulates the world according to his needs; he either walks to the well, thereby eliminating his need by gratification, or he communicates his requirements by gestures or verbalization. After his organismic balance is

From Planned Psychotherapy to Gestalt Therapy

restored, however, his interest is free for other activities, and his friend's promotion can become figure, that is, it can become a reality, can jump into existence.

On your camera you have a view finder. This view finder, in contrast to the ancient cumbersome direct observation on a frosted glass, facilitates the taking of pictures considerably. The human organism has a corresponding system at its disposal, it has what we call a mind, or, rather, different strata of minds, of which the sensoro-motoric one is the most primitive. If there is no environment present, which according to the figure/background function can become reality, we visualize, daydream, night dream, or even archaically hallucinate the situation required for the satisfaction of our needs. It is obvious that such a situation corresponds to Freud's term of wishful thinking, But the later developed mind systems of semantic appraisal and of higher abstractions provide us with better means of orientation than the senso-motoric mind which is a mere, though often valuable, concrete indicator of our needs. The higher mind system which includes many functions commonly known as thinking, is a combination of orientation and manipulation in minute doses. It selects, rejects, combines, it recalls past experiences, in short, it does what your school has recognized as the function of the dream. It attempts solutions of unfinished situations.

I have called this process an instinct cycle. The instinct cycle shows a cause and a purpose. The cause is the disturbance — for instance, dehydration — which upsets the organismic equilibrium, and the purpose is the regaining of this equilibrium. The links connecting cause and achievement are the figure/background/formation, tensions or drives — in our case thirst — intelligence, efficiency and character. Intelligence is the adequate functioning of the orientative, efficiency that of the motoric system. They together form the pattern of behavior which finally integrates into character and personality.

From Planned Psychotherapy to Gestalt Therapy

I have described the working of the organism as if it were essentially spontaneous with little room left for deliberate activity — for instance, planning. It has to be emphasized that at this stage the deliberate activity works harmoniously in the service of the organism, enhancing and not destroying its survival value.

The picture changes with acculturation. Rulers, privileged classes and other social factors introduce taboos and commandments. Moralism ascends the throne. willpower is glorified and deliberate action demanded. But this deliberate activity is essentially a saying "No!" to *many instinct* cycles, undermining the biological foundation of man, degenerating him and finally bringing about the process which we have the dubious pleasure of witnessing, namely the rapid loss of man's survival value. This is only too clearly shown by the rapidly rising curves of mental and psychosomatic illness and the spreading insurance mentality — the cry for ever increasing security. With such a somber orientation, what is one to do? Can we arrest or even reverse the vicious circle?

The fact that the U.S.A. is becoming psychiatrically minded, is a hope and a danger. In this state of emergency, analysis of many years duration are a luxury, and brief therapy does not create integrated personalities which alone can guaranty the survival of mankind.

The American government is beginning to plan, so far rather chaotically, an attack on the personality disorders, and as far as education and group therapy are concerned, some valuable work in the mental hygiene field has commenced. But what about the treatment situation?

Like many others, I have tried to find a method to shorten the time required for psychoanalysis, all the time keeping in mind that I must not sacrifice thoroughness, but I may possibly increase its efficiency. My own experiences with the Freudian School, and the many wasted years, had taught me how to avoid many mistakes.

From Planned Psychotherapy to Gestalt Therapy

But this was not enough. I saw the classical analysis in the light of the first cumbersome and clumsy electrical machine, and saw that one could — to use an Americanism — streamline the psychotherapeutic method. I got much orientation from the Gestalt psychological and semantic trends of thought. Finally I came to a ridiculously simple theory: if the Neurotic is a dissociated personality, one has only to collect all the dissociated parts of the personality and to reintegrate them. On account of its haziness and inconsistency, I had to discard the libido theory; I could not accept its stickiness as cement to glue the dissociated properties together. So I let the death instinct take charge of the libido, turned away from my worship of the gods Eros and Thanatos, and tried to find new bearings. Man is in continuity with nature and therefore obeys the laws of nature. Modern physics has discovered that isolated *energies* do not exist *but are functions of matter*. Thus I look for functions and not for energies. I believe I was successful in my search. Integration turned out to be largely a matter of assimilation and contact, aggression a function of manipulation, especially in the service of the alimentary needs. Thoughts, symptoms, memories, habits, were biological processes. With the new outlook I managed to achieve a good deal of integration within myself. From then on the road was easy, for there is a great thing about being an integrated, unitary individual, namely: integration facilitates its own development, just as dissociation arrests or even reverses individual development.

This finding provides us with a clear indication of when to finish psychoanalytical treatment. As soon as the patient has achieved that integration which facilitates its own development we can safely leave him to himself. We can perhaps also use this criterion as a maxim for child education and tentatively say: the child does not want affection, it even hates being suffocated with it. The child wants facilitation, that is, opportunity and assistance for his development.

From Planned Psychotherapy to Gestalt Therapy

At this point you probably expect me to elaborate on the ways in which my outlook on the human personality differs from other psychoanalytical concepts. Unfortunately, I must disappoint you. Such a detailed account — beyond what can be gauged from what I have said so far — would take many hours, and I am afraid I have already trespassed sufficiently on your patience. However, I would like to say something about the practical application of these ideas.

Basically, I am applying a push and pull method. I give integration exercises to my patients according to the nature and severity of their dissociation. I know quite well that they cannot do these exercises in an efficient manner, so, as we go along, we analyze the difficulties or resistances step by step.

In this respect to planning, I do not differ much from other psychotherapists. If he is a Freudian and thinks that the neurosis is the outcome of a childhood amnesia, his plan will be to make conscious the whole childhood, and he will set out in his pursuit with his tool of free dissociations, or flight of ideas. Another will search for inconsistencies in the character formation, forgetting the biological substratum and treating the character as something isolated from the organism as a whole, something similar to the religious soul concept. If he is an Adlerian he will systematically pump self-assurance into the patient, raising the level of his confidence. If he believes in external influences he will apply suggestions, if the crux lies with the orgonon he will set free vegetative energies with the perfect orgasm as the goal. If semantic blockages are the scapegoat he will employ the "structural differential" for the cure.

I believe that my concept, in that it considers the organism as a whole is more comprehensive and therefore on the whole more efficient than the methods just mentioned, and except for Reich's and Korzybski's approach, more methodical. As my theory assumes that the basic human functions are orientation and manipulation, every interference with the biological instinct cycles will maintain

From Planned Psychotherapy to Gestalt Therapy

the specific dissociation by diminishing awareness or disturbing the free use of the motoric system. Our patients are desensitized or awkward or both.

The fact that one can achieve results with psychotherapy at all is explained by a very important factor: one often reads about repression of instincts. Such assumption is wrong. Instincts probably can never be repressed. This would result in a changed constitution. What can be repressed is their expression and gratification. The figure/background/formation can be interfered with by deliberately changing one's attention, recognition of one's needs by blotting out awareness, for instance, by amnesia, scotomization, frigidity, semantic blockage, and so on, expression and gratification by linguistic and other motoric blockages, such as paralysis, and, more often, muscular spasms.

To dissolve these pathological interferences, I rely upon the patient's detailed descriptions of his experiences and my own observation, and try to use as little construction and guesswork — for instance interpretation — as possible, and endeavor to stick to the reality of the analytical situation.

For Freud, the reality principle had the meaning of sensible adjustment to society. Freud, as has been repeatedly pointed out, especially by members of this group, had too rigid a view of society in general and paid insufficient attention to the diversity of the individual environment in particular.

To me reality is actuality. The past exists no more and the future not yet. Both Freud, with his emphasis on causes and on the past, and Adler, with his stress on goal seeking and concern with the future, miss the balance of the present tense.

About a month ago, I had a shocking experience. After years of psychoanalytical treatment, first with a leading, and later with another, analyst of the classical school, a lady came to me in a rather bad state. During her narration she twice jerked as if experiencing an intense fright. Both times it happened when she dared to utter some doubt. I asked her what her analyst had to say about these jerks. Her answer was: "He never noticed them." However, were I to tackle these analysts about their procedure, they would maintain that of course they start with the present situation. Perhaps they do. If I have one grain of bread for breakfast, I can still say I have eaten something. I may add that she is now quickly recovering from her psychoanalysis.

As the first step towards integrating, I advocate the reawakening of the sense of actuality or reality, the experiencing of the self and the world. The neurotic has a diminished contact with reality. Side by side with avoidance of the company of others, and escape into intellectualism, we frequently find the flight into the past, the looking for so-called causes and explanations and other avoidances of responsibility, or we find the jump into the future, for instance in daydreams or waiting for rewards from heaven — pie in the sky.

A patient of mine spent the first year and a half in treatment telling his analyst about his difficult wife, his disappointing friends, and his business troubles. He dutifully associated to the different people and brought up a lot of material. The actual situation, however, namely the psychoanalytical situation, had a specific significance. As he complained to me about these people, I made him listen to his wailing voice and we discussed the fact that he avoided the tackling of the different people, which would mean personal contact with them, and instead always complained to one person about some other.

I often like to start with a pedantic exercise: I ask the patient to start every sentence with the word "now" or even "here and now," as "now I am lying on a couch, now I don't know what to say, now I feel my heart beating, now I am thinking of the quarrel I had yesterday with my wife." In the last remarks, the connection between his experiencing a slight anxiety attack and talking about the rela-

From Planned Psychotherapy to Gestalt Therapy

tion with his wife is obvious. Often, however, the patient will escape from experiencing the present. He will go into the past or the future, especially if he has had a drill in the Freudian or Adlerian method respectively. I maintain that the past is of significance only as far as it embodies unfinished situations — for instance — undigested experiences. The futuristic thinking also becomes pathological if, instead of being aware of the present deficiencies, the patient drugs himself with "if's" and other forms of daydreams. We always dream in the present tense, we experience a dream as an actuality. The knowledge of this phenomenon is often applied in hypnosis by making the patient go back, as if traveling in a Wellsian time engine, to the place and time of the past. Such a procedure can be used without any hypnotical complications. Try it on yourself. Go back to any place of your childhood and simply describe in great detail what you actually visualize. You will be astonished what a lot of forgotten material you will recover.

After the patient has grasped the concept of the "now," I usually drop the word "now" and acquaint him with my formulation of the basic rule which says that he should convey to me everything he does and experiences intellectually, emotionally and physically, that he should neither hold back anything deliberately, nor force himself to say something that he dislikes expressing. He should indicate only that there is something he does not want to or cannot reveal.

As you recognize, the last part of the basic rule allows for the dealing with the censor and the discussion of the different forms of emotional resistances, like embarrassment, fear, disgust, politeness, and so on.

The first part of the rule is, as far as I can see, comprehensive, especially if you bear in mind that thinking is orientation and manipulation in minute doses, that thinking is invisible action. At that stage, the phenomenon of running away into the past or future with the loss of reference to the present, serves as a good indication of the extent to which the patient is willing or capable of co-operating. The general pattern of his interpersonal relationship is also coming readily into the analytical situation. He will be slavishly obedient, or making fun of the procedure, he will be cooperative on the surface but leading the rule ad absurdum, he will talk *about* the rule instead of complying with it. However, after he has had experiences which shake him to the core, then his not complying always indicates considerable resistance which he slowly learns to recognize.

I shall briefly relate two cases demonstrating extremes in co-operation.

One is a woman of about forty, a social worker with the ambition to become a psychoanalyst. She talks a highfalutin language with technical terms replacing content. She is a coarse type, but suffers from the delusion that she is a lady, born for higher purposes in life. For a long time I could do nothing except persistently try to persuade her to attempt the basic exercise. She would insist that this was a waste of time, or she would be bored, or enumerate the contents of the room. She did not feel anything beyond an occasional heart beating. She was, in other words, deeply desensitized and intellectualized, if you can call her *dementia verbosa* intellect. One day, however, it was the fourteenth hour with me, she came in with a notebook in which she had mapped out prescriptions of how I should conduct the analysis. When she lay on the couch, she always lay in a closed position, but that day she opened up a bit, and after a time became very restless and even became aware of this. Finally she burst into tears and said: "I feel like a ship which is tossed about by everybody. I must keep my superiority, otherwise I am lost." This first breakthrough took fourteen hours — however, as a breakthrough it did not amount to anything. On the contrary, she even became more difficult and was on the verge of giv-

From Planned Psychotherapy to Gestalt Therapy

ing up. As I am not in the habit of blaming a patient and making her responsible for her resistances, I had to look for my own deficiency, and I found the following facts: I was personally involved in her case. She had to be a feather in my cap, she was a test of whether or not I was capable of handling such difficult cases. That means that I had lost the analytical objectivity and had made her a tool of my ambition. Instead of dealing with the present only, I had become involved in futuristic or purposive thinking. I further noticed this: when she produced her suggestions, I had felt angry, that this pipsqueak wanted to tell me how to go about my business. This anger was an indication that somehow she must be right. She could and did teach me something: namely, that I had slipped up on my own theory, that instead of looking at the actuality of her symptom, of her need for being top dog, I had reacted to it.

Then I let her live through her needs for making suggestions, demands on people. This finally crystallized in the demand of being accepted under any condition. I then explained to her that she wanted to be accepted, but that she was not willing to accept me and my way of dealing with her, what's more — that she was not willing to accept her own emotions. She is now beginning to show insight into her neurotic conflict, into her struggle between the artificial facade and the emotional self which she fears.

The contrasting case has had five hours so far. He is a philosophy student who was said to be schizoid. He came to analysis because life had lost its flavor, he could not concentrate any more, and he had thoughts of suicide. He is homosexual, but is no longer practicing it. Philosophically, he was interested in the Aristotelian approach, but lately he has become interested in Husserl and somewhat in the French school of existentialism.

As my approach is somewhat similar to Husserl's phenomenology, he had no difficulty in grasping the meaning of my approach, and after the first half hour I could introduce the next step

— the dealing with processes. Whilst in the beginning it is sufficient for the patient to realize that something quote "is" unquote, there, later he must realize that something is going on, or rather on and on and on. He has to get acquainted with the fact that his experiences, his behavior, his symptoms, his thoughts, and so on, are *processes* or time-space events. They have duration. He has to learn to concentrate on his symptom, to follow up the development that takes place when he is in contact with the symptom, when he is re-sensitizing and re-mobilizing it.

Here is a part of the third hour. He relates: "The front of my head is aching, my mouth is dry, my head wants to push back into the pillow. Now I am breathless. I see myself running down the street. A motor car is running over me, but does not touch me. I don't know whether this really happened. My knees are very heavy, my eyes want to close, I feel as if I want to cry, but can't. I have not cried for six years." Then he starts talking about his father who was run over by a motor car and killed. He relates this and the details of the accident and death in a matter of fact voice. The moment, however, he visualizes the coffin, he bursts into a loud, intense, and genuine crying.

The same patient has a syndrome which one can best tackle by home exercises. These home exercises are an important factor in the shortening of the treatment. Although the classical analysis demands that the patient should only submit himself to the analysis and that he should stop *doing* things, the Freudian analyst will welcome the patient's finding out something about himself or, in a case of agoraphobia, his making attempts to cross the street. So why not plan and organize the co-operation of the patient, or, in case of unconscious sabotage or compulsive dummy activity, use this for the mobilization of his resistance awareness?

Our philosophy student has lost his contact with and the liking of his environment. As far as I can see this always goes hand in

From Planned Psychotherapy to Gestalt Therapy

hand with a dead palate. He does not enjoy or taste his food. He enjoys eating only when he has cooked something for another person and the other likes it. In a case like this I give eating exercises, starting with observations of the amount of attention the patient gives to his eating. Is he reading or day-dreaming during the meal? Does he gulp his food down, in other words, drink even solid food?

After the fifth session, he has already begun to taste his food and correspondingly life starts to become interesting again. He begins to go about and resumes contact with friends. Although on the whole, he is still very wooden in his speech, some loosening up of his emotional life such as a slight smile, can already be seen.

If a patient has desensitized his visualization and has, instead of pictures, only words in his mind, I try to develop his interest in noticing his environment instead of merely abstracting from it. At the same time, I aim at dissolving the reluctance to face the world and form an impression of it.

The female patient mentioned before has a complete blockage in regard to visualization. At present there is no question yet of embarking on such tasks, as she is interested only in how the world looks at *her*.

A very intelligent and conscientious instructor came for analysis for his sexual impotence. Fie took quickly to the concentration technique. After very few sessions he wriggled on the couch in a peculiar way which he recognized as a struggle he had had with his mother, when at the age of nine, she forced him to lie still while she removed some worms or something from his genitals. In the following sessions his movements changed and we followed them up with interpretations. However, the fact that he interpreted so easily, and that he was well acquainted with Reich's work, made me suspicious. Perhaps he was living up to his expectation of Reichian analysis. I also was not willing to give up so quickly my

From Planned Psychotherapy to Gestalt Therapy

opinion about the decisive importance of the actuality situation. Finally he produced a symptom of restlessness which did not cease and which for the first time he himself could not interpret. He could not settle down on the coach, He kept one or even two shoulders away from the cover. This looked to me like a wrestling position. He confirmed this impression. He remembered a fight where he had resisted similarly. The symptom, or rather, his body language persisted, until I asked him if by any chance this symbolized his attitude towards me. And then he let go. We had had an argument some time before about experimental psychology, and he'd been damned if he would submit to my viewpoint. After my question: "Could we not agree to disagree?" he calmed down and for the first time settled down comfortably.

In the majority of patients, the direct attack on the desensitization and immobilization, provides no difficulty. On the contrary, the patients realize soon that something is going on; they see painful and uncomfortable symptoms disappear or rather change into a feeling of well being. In all these cases a certain contact with the self had survived in spite of rigid self control.

However, at least three types require the prolonged spadework of intense character analysis before one can attempt the phenomenological analysis. In these types, one finds a deep seated contempt for their spontaneous personalities, a rejection of "what is" and a glorification of "what should be." These people hanker after ideals. They have alienated their own feelings and needs to such an extent, that under no circumstances must they recognize and still less accept their selves.

Besides the one type mentioned earlier, there is the "as if" personality — to use a term coined by Helene Deutsch. Patients of this type assume roles and will with pseudo-compliance deceive the analyst just as they bluff their way through life in general. Not before they realize the fact that they are always on stage, that they

From Planned Psychotherapy to Gestalt Therapy

have not a character armor, but a wardrobe full of costumes will they come out with their true nature. This step is usually accompanied by a feeling of great emptiness and sensation seeking. There is one symptom which often heralds the existence of an "as if" personality — chronic boredom. As you probably know, boredom sets in when your attention is deliberately given to a situation in which you are not interested, and when, at the same time, the natural figure/background/formation is blocked. The "as if" personality, instead of giving in to the f/b/f, tries to overcome boredom by ever-increasing addiction to thrills and sometimes to drugs.

Another type that provides great initial difficulty is one of the obsessional types. I am not referring to the conscientious, systematizing, perhaps over-systematizing hard-working type. He is highly cooperative. But there is another obsessional character who is mostly conscious of a fear of being made a fool of. He indulges in unconstructive dummy activities in his mind, as well as in his life. He is always serious, but never sincere. With him, the initial difficulty lies in making him aware of the fact that he has one aim — to gather secret triumphs. He will lead your demands ad absurdum, argue for hours, frustrate you and demonstrate that you are an impotent ass, incapable of dealing with such a clever chap as he is. But he has projected his fooling, and imagines that other people want to make a fool out of him. He fails to realize that he is the one who is out to fool everybody. Only after he can realize what a fool he is to spend his life with fooling about will he settle down to sincere work and cooperation.

Perhaps one can also include in this category a type that is often distinguished by its valuable contribution to society. This is the person who always has to justify his existence. You know that a man who has to prove his sexual potency is not very sure about it. You find a similar structure in the person who feels the need of justifying his existence. He does not exist fully. He is, like the other three types enumerated before, desensitized to such a degree that intellectual and social goals have to replace the unfelt biological drives. Without his constructed aims he would feel as empty as the other types. Marx once said that the existence of a phenomenon proves its requirements. Without the American neurosis, psycho-analysis would quickly die in the States. Similarly the French philo-sophical movement of existentialism derives its *raison d'etre* from our rapidly dwindling self-awareness.

Alcoholism presents a very interesting contribution to our theme. It is a futile attempt to solve the conflict between self-ex-pression and desensitization. Drinking assists in the emotional dis-charge — thus lowering unbearable tensions, but the conscience or ideal, as well as the feeling of unworthiness and self-consciousness, are desensitized only temporarily. The alcoholic, like other neurot-ics, has failed to surrender his individuality to society, he has not adjusted himself to society's demand that he become a well-be-haved robot.

I must finish. I cannot go into the details of all the different forms of dimming orientation and manipulation. I have to omit the very interesting connection between the numbness of the alimen-tary functions and the paranoid phenomenon, between retroflect-ion and repression, between Ego development and contact func-tion, and many other occurrences dealing with awareness distur-bances, but I can roughly sketch the course which the average treatment takes:

In the fore-field we find the character as a safeguard of the status quo. After working through the main characterological resis-tance, the patient learns to experience himself again. The main point in this experiencing himself is the optimum of awareness, the discrimination between pathological introspection and intensified existence. Through experiencing his personal processes, he is be-coming aware of his split into deliberate, suppressive and a sponta-

From Planned Psychotherapy to Gestalt Therapy

neous, suppressed personality. During this time he identifies with the suppressing part, which tries to dissociate itself by all means, for instance by muscular contractions, from the unacceptable part of his personality. At that stage his interpersonal relations are colored by his fears of not being acceptable to his environment. In the next stage, his self-control, self-reproaches, self-punishment, has to be redirected towards the environment, thus multiplying his contact possibility with his enemies and friends. Deliberately he begins to control, reproach, punish, them. This redirecting enables him to finish many conflicts which, by internalization, had become permanent. He changes self reproach into object approach. By identifying with all his processes, he is slowly learning to accept his spontaneous personality. With the disappearance of his internal conflicts, he becomes sufficiently strong and unified to regard his opinions as of equal importance as those of others. Instead of living in continuous fear of being rejected, and need to be accepted, *he* is now doing the accepting and rejecting. He takes just as much from the world as he is willing and capable of assimilating for his future development. Whilst in the pre-treatment period he had accepted and rejected people for being good or bad, he discriminates now situations and properties, he develops a taste of his own and manipulates the world toward an optimum of collective satisfaction. Deliberateness changes from authoritarian self-control into liberal self-and object-management.

I hope that I was able to show that neurosis is an unbiological attempt of solving man's social problems. It acts in the pattern of the biblical "If an eye offends thee tear it out." The result is a limited instead of a wholesome personality.

The reintegration of the dissociated parts of the personality is best undertaken by re-sensitizing and re-mobilizing the system of orientation and manipulation. As far as I can see, this program is comprehensive. By experiencing his symptoms, et cetera, as processes, the patient acquires the awareness and conscious control required for his semantic and social adjustment — that is, the understanding of his personal needs and the manipulation of his environment. These processes are actually taking place and must therefore be dealt with in the present as the balancing point between past and future. The reorganizing of the personality consists of both disintegrating and integrating processes, and should be balanced so that only such amount of dissociated material should be set free as the patient is capable of assimilating. Otherwise his social or even biological function may be dangerously upset.

The analytical disintegrative process concerns infantile and irrational orientation, uneconomical and rigid manipulation, emotional and semantic blockages. The integrative processes are the recognizing and assimilating of traumatic, introjected and projected material, the functions of contact and emotionally and semantically adequate self-expression.

As soon as the structure of the neurosis is clear to the therapist, he should plan his course of action, but remain alert and elastic during the whole treatment.

I do not want to conclude this paper without mentioning one point of danger: between the one-sided approaches, namely, between the purely psychologistic concept of Korzybski, Adler, and Horney, and the biologistic method of the schools of F. M. Alexander and Elsa Gindler; between the analytical technique of Freud, and the creative endeavor of, say, a music teacher; between Reich's sexualized personality and Jung's desexualized libido. In the midst of all these abstractions of the complete personality, there is enough room, even the need, left, for these and many more forms of operation. The other danger involved is eclecticism. Instead of having a comprehensive and Unitary point of view and operation right in the center, one might jump from one method to another

From Planned Psychotherapy to Gestalt Therapy

and back again, spreading confusion and producing merely a different type of dissociated personality.

The safeguard against such a danger is the concept and experience of the human personality as being an indivisible whole and as always embedded in, and related to an environmental personal and social field. As your society starts just from this, assumption, the danger of succumbing to such eclecticism is slight. On the contrary, if I may make a suggestion, I recommend as necessary complementary aspects of the study of the human personality at least three subjects: Gestalt psychology, semantics, and last but not least the approach of the Gindler School.

Finally I would like to make some personal remarks: I wish to express my gratitude to you for having given me the opportunity to voice my point of view.

After many years of struggling on my own in Africa with the Freudian ideas, I came to some conclusions. Although Freud was the Livingstone of the Unconscious, the map which he had drawn had already become antiquated. It did not represent any more a true means of guidance, it had to be redrawn. I believed I had found some relevant points of orientation, but many blanks — for instance, what constitutes awareness — were still left. So I had come to a place where my drawing could be checked and where I could possibly get some of the blanks filled. As the point of gravity of science has shifted to the U.S.A., your country was the obvious goal. In South Africa, I was considered a megalomaniac rebel for daring to contradict the words of the master; in Canada, a fool for doubting the sacrosanct reflex arc; in New Haven, a stray dog for wanting to do psychotherapy without a medical license, and, what's more, without belonging to an established group; in New York a plain lunatic for having abandoned a secure economical position. Something had to be wrong with me, or I had to have an ulterior motive. Of course, I understand, I cannot attack the roots

From Planned Psychotherapy to Gestalt Therapy

of a man's credo and, at the same time expect to be accepted, but I knew that I was not merely destructive, but constructive and instructive as well. Was I so completely mistaken or were all of them blind? Then a miracle happened to me. A few months ago I met some members of your group, and I was deeply moved as I had been seldom in my life. After all, there were people on this globe who saw the world as I saw it, who spoke a language similar to mine. It was like a dream, nearly too good to be true. I felt like a sailor who knew he was steering the right course, but became weary that he would never see land again, and suddenly, unexpectedly, there it was. But this was not all, this must not be all. The great tide of man's disintegration, of mankind's suicide is coming in. Dykes have to be built. Could we do it together? Could the hope that it may not be too late, turn into possibility?

Freud started with the neurotic as an exceptional case amidst a healthy environment. I believe, however, that neurosis has become an all embracing social phenomenon. Thus the question I have to put before you is: Is the time ripe to attack this social illness on a scale different from our present piecemeal approach? Can or should one plan psychotherapy on a grand scale? I personally doubt that society and administration are ready to see the severity of the problem, but I have the impression that they are no more completely desensitized to the existence of the problem itself.

Freud saw only the discomfort in our culture. Spengler visualized the doom of the Occident. We witness just now the disintegration of Europe, but we witness something else as well. Previously, one culture could finish its cycle and disappear, and there was enough room on this globe for many more to come. But the world has shrunk, every nation is drawn into the orbit of the European-American culture cycle. Thus the end of this culture means the end of everything. A schizophrenic *weltuntergangs* fantasy, the fantasy of the world's doom, seems to become a reality.

From Planned Psychotherapy to Gestalt Therapy

It was not a scientist, but a poet, who has seen this first. It was
D. H. Lawrence who said:

"... Connie laughed. The rain was pouring down.
'He hated them!'
'No,' said he. 'He didn't bother. He just disliked them.
There's a difference. Because,' as he said, 'the Tommies
are getting just as priggish and narrow-gutted. It's the
fate of mankind to go that way.'"

Theory and Technique of Personality Integration

Reprinted from American Journal of Psychotherapy, *Vol. 2, No.4, October 1948*

This was Perls's first article to appear in a professional journal in the United States. He again makes reference to the Gestalt psychologists and makes references to the "body" therapists of the time — Wilhelm Reich, F. M. Alexander and Elsa Gindler — whose work would have an important impact on the impending theoretical development of Gestalt therapy.

In the development of man from the lower animal to his present stage, there occurred at least three events of decisive interest especially for the psychotherapist. The first was the development of the cortex specific for the Homo sapiens. For the first time an animal acquired faculties different from those which other animals developed in the struggle for survival. The human brain developed the faculty of delaying responses and thus modulating instinctive behavior, and made possible the consulting of previous experiences. This resulted in the development of tools and deliberate

From Planned Psychotherapy to Gestalt Therapy

action; in other words, at that stage deliberateness supported the spontaneous instinctive behavior in the pursuit of gratification of man's organismic needs and his defenses.

The second stage began when man was required to use his deliberateness not for the support but for the harnessing of instinctive behavior. This occurred at a time when the survival of society assumed more importance than the survival of the individual. However, the instincts were merely harnessed and channeled; there was no tendency to eliminate them as something evil.

The third period began with Greek philosophy, when man became conscious of himself as an object and when he discovered the "mind." Beginning with the Christian notion of the "sin of thought," man then turned his will power against himself, forgetting more and more that the organismic needs are the very soil on which he thrives. Dichotomy was born, and it has reached in our time a stage where it defeats its own purpose. The individual in our time lives no more for the benefit of society of which he is a part but for the sake of the production of machines and money. Personal development is, like initiative and many other primary characteristics, projected. The fetish of our time is industrial development, a development in which the workman is more and more required to be an automaton. He produces machine-made parts which, and this is of decisive importance, must show no variation. In this process, the individual and society are rapidly losing their survival value.

The dichotomy of the human personality can be approached from three angles: From the point of view of the dualistic structure of *personality*, of the dualistic *behavior*, and of the dualistic *language*. Man could regain his survival value if these dualisms could be reintegrated, if he could create a unitary language and a sufficient number of unitary personalities. Individually, we are already capable of doing the latter, but we are far from producing unitary personalities on the conveyor belt. The essential requirement for reintegration would be the production of an adequate tool, and this instrument would have to be the unitary language.

Leonardo da Vinci, Goethe, Freud and Einstein started with the structure of events and kept up the primary contact with the nonverbal world, verbalizing only *a posteriori* what they had found. How different is the approach of most of us! We *begin* with words. We hear "complex," "repression," "libido," "obsession," "schizoid." Then we try to grasp the meanings of those words and go out on our search to find the confirming facts. We shout enthusiastically, "Freud is right! These things *do* exist." Or, if we do not like what we find, we become para-Freudians, accepting bits and pieces here and there and rejecting others. But if we have enough discrimination left and if we do not simply swallow the collected works — those millions of words — we can still hope for progress. However, we must not get stuck in the morass of our own theories. We must not be deceived by the double-tongued, glib, compartmental thinkers who tell us at one moment that the master himself regarded his ideas as mere theories, and at the next moment react with indignation when we have ideas of our own about "libido" and some other treasured labels of their jargon.

Because of the significance of the language problem, it is important that we try to understand it. What makes language so attractive and so concealing? Can one conceive a means-whereby we can penetrate the linguistic veil that hides reality? Shall we return to our belief in magic or shall we denounce the effectiveness of language altogether? Finally, is our language adequate to the task which we have undertaken; namely, the integration, or rather the reintegration, of human beings?

Our present-day language seems to be a totally inadequate instrument for our undertaking. If this is true, how handicapped we are! After all, language is our professional tool, and certainly, any

From Planned Psychotherapy to Gestalt Therapy

craftsman is seriously handicapped by poor tools. While the surgeon is improving his technique, the physicist building better cyclotrons, the general practitioner using more efficient drugs, the farmer modernizing his implements, we still try to do the impossible: to integrate personalities with the help of a non-integrative language. A unitary language which would create, or result from, unitary personalities is a condition *sine qua non* for an integrated personal or social structure; but today the development of such a language is in its infancy. (Among others, Korzybski and L. L. White have concerned themselves with the creation of a unitary language.)

At present we are dissociated, dualistic personalities with a dualistic language, a dualistic mentality, a dualistic existence. The deep split in our personality, the conflict between deliberate and spontaneous behavior, is the outstanding characteristic of our time. Our civilization is characterized by technical integration and personality deterioration. The statistics of industrial production and of personality disorder show a parallel increase.

If the assumption is correct that the split personality is the normal, perhaps even unavoidable product of our time, doubt arises as to whether or not an integration is possible, or if so, whether or not it has market value or at least survival value. If an integrated personality, or as I prefer to call it, a unitary person should have a unitary language, how much of an understanding between him and those who use the present-day dualistic language could be achieved?

The examples of Heraclitus, Spinoza, Bach, and Goethe, who were such unitary personalities, are evidence that this is not merely a fantastic goal. On the other hand, Freud, like Beethoven, was a dualistic giant. He produced an apparently balanced scientific system of opposing energies even at the cost of having to introduce his mysterious death instinct, but he did not achieve that degree of unification of his own personality which would have seen dualities as different aspects of the same phenomenon and not as irreconcilable contradictions.

Let us look at some of the prevailing dualisms, for instance the conception of "body and mind." Philosophers tried to glue the two together in a psycho-physical parallelism. Illnesses are made out to have either psychological or organic causes. In the unitary concept of the organism-as-a-whole, the "body" becomes the visible aspect of the personality while the "mind" appears as a number of functions, especially as attention, which means as a subject-object relationship.

"God and World" is another dualistic concept in the conviction of most believers. The integration which Spinoza accomplished was premature; it had no decisive social consequences. In contrast, present-day society accepts the integration of time and space, of mass and velocity, as a *timely* expression of our quantitative-century, and Einstein's theory of relativity is-at least for the time being — a valid unitary interpretation.

Let us compare Freud's concept of "libido" with that of "attraction." "Libido" as opposed to "aggression" is dualistic; a unification cannot be brought about by integration, but only by behaving like a young dog that tries to bite its own tail. Thus it is not astonishing that we meet in the Freudian language monstrosities like "aggressive libido" and "latent negative transference."

"Attraction" belongs to the unitary approach. It is not irreconcilably opposed to "separation"; both expressions mean movement of a body in relation to a field. Thus Karen Horney's ideas about "moving-toward" and "moving-away" types have integrative value. Freud himself saw the antithetical meaning of many root words; e.g., the Latin *"altus"* which we translate with either "high" or "low." He saw the dialectical relationship of a number of processes like sadism and masochism, but in more decisive concepts he retained his dualistic outlook. After he had crystallized, and thereby

From Planned Psychotherapy to Gestalt Therapy

solidified, his system, it was completed, and no further development can be expected from there.

Alfred Adler was the first to outgrow Freud's system. He saw how one-sidedly Freud had looked at the past and at causes, but he himself was equally prejudiced, overemphasized the future and purposiveness. Wilhelm Reich refused to accept Freud's vague notions on the means-whereby a repression takes place. He found the answer in the muscular tensions coexistent with every neurosis and called the totality of these spasms the motor armor.

The general trend however, seems to go away from the biological foundations of our existence and instead stresses the characterological aspect and our situation within society (as if a character were put on like the mask in Greek tragedy, and as if we were not society ourselves). Security and adjustment seem to be more important than personality development.

The problem we have to face can now be formulated: How can we achieve the transition from the split into the unified personality, from the dualistic to a unitary language, from the antithetical to a truly comprehensive philosophy?

We should not underestimate either the importance or the difficulty of the task. A progressive dichotomy threatens the survival of mankind. Whether or not mankind is committing suicide or preparing for a more adequate form of existence, nobody can tell at this time. The latter would have to be a reintegrate existence, not an artificially glued-together edifice of incoherent approaches. It entails the acceptance of the organism-as-a-whole with the sincerity of William Alanson White or Kurt Goldstein and not with the lip-service which so many of the present-day movements pay to this concept. Their unitary outlook is blocked by blind spots. They have a piece of the cake and imagine that they have the whole. Their personality is crippled, and their organism-as-a-whole con-

From Planned Psychotherapy to Gestalt Therapy

cept corresponds to the specific aspect of themselves which they permit to exist.

The concept of the organism-as-a-whole is the center of the gestalt psychological approach which is superseding the mechanistic association psychology. New York, which as no other place in the world has many different movements attempting to come to grips with psychotherapy, also attracted the three great gestalt psychologists, Koehler, Wertheimer and Kurt Goldstein. Goldstein broke with the rigid concept of the reflex arc. According to him, both kinds of nerves, the sensor and the motor, stretch from the organism to the environment. The concept that sensing is a passive, mechanistic phenomenon has to be replaced by the insight that we are active and selective in our sensing. I have called the sensory apparatus our means of orientation and the motor one that of manipulation. With this linguistic adjustment, the senses, far from being purely mechanical means for the transport of acoustic and other waves, become once more an aspect of personality itself. Thus the vista is open for an approach in which an individual may again come to his senses.

Now we meet on familiar ground. The senses are the means of awareness, consciousness, attention. Lack of awareness is characteristic for the neurotic. Insufficient awareness of past traumatic experiences has been considered by Freud as the cause of the neurosis. Frigidity and scotoma are two more examples of diminished awareness. I have studied extensively the corresponding phenomena of the alimentary tract.

Quite briefly, my theory is the following: Difficult situations create wishful and magic thinking, scientific manipulation, propaganda, and the philosophy of the free will: in short, deliberateness in place of spontaneity. Human behavior, as far as it was and is objectionable to a person or a group, has to be changed. But "goody-goody" behavior does not replace, but only supersedes the

From Planned Psychotherapy to Gestalt Therapy

spontaneous attitude. Instincts as the source of unwanted behavior cannot be eliminated, only their expressions can be modified or annihilated. Generally, it is the expression and execution of the organismic needs, of the biological, original personality which is scotomized and paralyzed. Consequently; the modem individual has to be re-sensitized and re-mobilized in order to achieve integration.

If we set out with the idea of correlating the sensory-motor nervous system to orientation and manipulation, we arrive at an unbroken chain of interdependencies which begins with the rapid automatic reaction, the so-called reflex, and progresses to the delayed responses of medium and high order. A convenient example of the medium order response is rifle shooting. A perfect and continuous coordinating of orientation and manipulation, a permanent adjustment to the changing situation, is required to hit a moving target. The property of the human brain to delay action is already pronounced in this example. Climbing up the ladder of abstractions, we come to the high-order activities of planning, blueprinting, theorizing, and finally, to philosophizing. Every theory, every philosophy is a map from which we take our orientation for our actions. An adequate map is one that represents reality as truthfully as possible at any particular time. However, if one opens an atlas one finds all kinds of maps; some give an orientation about the geography of a country, others tell about the political or ethnographic situation. In addition, one can get information about wind movements, data on economics, or whatever aspect of reality one is interested in.

In other words, reality *per se* does not exist for the human being. It is something different for each individual, for each group, for each culture. Reality is determined by the individual's specific interests and needs.

From Planned Psychotherapy to Gestalt Therapy

Everything is in flux. Only after we have been stunned by the infinite diversity of processes constituting the universe can we understand the importance of the organizing principle that creates order from chaos; namely, the figure-background formation. Whatever is the organism's foremost need makes reality appear as it does. It makes such objects stand out as figures which correspond to diverse needs. It evokes our interest, attention, cathexis or whatever you choose to call it.

Bring the Sunday's *Herald Tribune* into a large family and watch the diversity of interests. Father seeks orientation in the business section, while mother skims the paper for basement bargains. Alec looks for instances of hardships of the suppressed classes, while Jack gets enthusiastic about a football game. Aunt Jenny indulges in the obituary columns, and the twins fight over the funnies.

The most important fact about the figure-background formation is that if a need is genuinely satisfied, the situation changes. The reality becomes a different one from what it was as long as the situation was unfinished. A neurosis is always characterized by the great number of unfinished situations. The patient is either not aware of them or is incapable of coping with them, which means that he is limited in his orientation or his manipulation or in both.

The healthy organism rallies with all its potentialities to the gratification of the foreground needs. Immediately as one task is finished it recedes into the background and allows the one which in the meantime has become the most important to come to the foreground. This is the principle of organismic self-regulation. Wilhelm Reich has dealt with this principle in connection with the orgasm and has contrasted it with the principle of moralistic regulation. I would prefer to call it the principle of deliberate regulation.

The psychotherapist's philosophy determines his specific approach. The priest will purify the soul with methods that increase

From Planned Psychotherapy to Gestalt Therapy

the awareness of the sinfulness of the forbidden deeds; the medicine man will attempt to change behavior by the use of bromides; the witch doctor will apply magic. The Freudian is concerned with the extraction of childhood traumata; the Adlerian with pumping confidence into his arrogant (inferiority-stricken) patient. If a school regards the inconsistencies of character as the root of all evil, it will endeavor to reconcile them; if the self-system is at fault, its stabilization will bring security into the interpersonal relations. If the perfect sexual orgasm produces the perfect personality, the therapeutic effort will be concentrated in that direction; and if incomplete awareness and immobility, as I suggest, are the scapegoats of the personality disorder, the method in question will be the re-sensitizing of the figure-background awareness and the re-mobilizing of all potentialities of the personality. This includes the harmonizing of both deliberate and spontaneous attitudes.

The ultimate goal of the treatment can be formulated thus: We have to achieve that amount of integration which facilitates its own development. This is in accordance with the fact that the dissociated person is inhibited or even degenerating in his development. To repeat once more, the criterion of a successful treatment is: *the achievement of that amount of integration which facilitates its own development.* A small hole cut into an accumulation of snow sometimes suffices to drain off the water. Once the draining has begun, the trickle broadens its bed by itself; it facilitates its own development. This facilitation of its own development should be given an important place in child education. The child requires, firstly, the gratification of its immediate needs and, secondly, the facilitation of its development.

But the child is, even with well-meaning parents, seldom given the facilitation of development of its inherent potentialities. It has to be shaped into something that finds the approval of parents and society. This entails two kinds of processes: the crippling of some attitudes and an artificial development of others. The spontaneous personality is being superseded by a deliberate one. On the behavior level we see the same dualism at work as we discussed previously in regard to the linguistic level. Spontaneity and deliberateness fight each other, producing conflicts, inconsistencies, distortions, discomfort in our civilization, while the integration of spontaneity and deliberateness could produce men capable of self-expression and self-realization.

Volition, conscience, living up to expectations, or whatever one chooses to call these deliberate attitudes, does not necessarily mean an inconsistency within the personality or a conflict with the environment, but it will lead to dichotomies if it is in conflict with the deeper layers of the personality, if it leads to the production and accumulation of unfinished situations within the personality. The unfinished situations cry for solutions, but if they are barred from awareness, neurotic symptoms and neurotic character formation will be the result.

Man is part of nature. He is a biological event; therefore, society is also part of nature. Speaking is a time-space event; so is thinking. Every abstract notion is as much a process as is the visualization of an object. Deliberate activity, self-control, conscience, are social and at the same time biological functions. Reintegration can be successful only if every human activity, deliberate as well as spontaneous, thoughts as well as instincts, are regarded and treated as biological processes.

Even at the risk of being redundant, this theme merits elaboration. A symptom is like a book, a precipitation of processes. The processes of observing, verbalizing, writing, selling, printing; the processes of making paper, ink, compositor's metal; the processes of distributing, advertising, and many more make up a book. Once it has become form it can partake in a variety of further processes. It can become a weapon to be thrown at one; an object to barter

From Planned Psychotherapy to Gestalt Therapy

for a bit of food; something with which to show off, or something to hide from parents; something to be burned by the Nazis; it can even become something to be read. In the latter case, the receptive processes are considerable and vary from staring at it to introjection, and even to digestion and assimilation.

Likewise, a neurotic symptom is the precipitation of processes; a hysterical headache, for instance, may be the end-result of being touchy, wanting to cry, being heroic about it, then squeezing the eye muscles until they hurt. Such a symptom can be used to get sympathy, an aspirin, or a thorough neurological examination. It can also be analyzed and its contributing processes integrated.

Functional and evolutional experimentation are the characteristics of global organic life. The baby is experimenting with sounds; the kitten with the strength of the branches it wants to climb. The schoolboy experiments with the teacher — how to cheat him or how to be in his good books. Once he has developed attitudes which appear to function adequately, he proceeds to other experiments.

The neurotic is always characterized by inadequate functions, mostly in the direction of unnecessary activity. This is most obvious in the obsessional type, but all neurotic character features are of a compulsive, rigid nature in contrast to the healthy experimental elastic attitude. The malfunctions of the neurotic become manifest in his lack of genuine self-expression. He cannot reveal himself before himself, and still less before others. His interpersonal relations as well as his development will, consequently, more and more deteriorate.

What technique is at present available to integrate the personalities of our patients: that is, to restore the organismic balance and to open the way for productive self-realization?

Freud's experiments with hysteria made him finally reject the hypnotic technique and develop a procedure which is now rigidly followed by the classical school. His pioneering spirit is found in the unorthodox rather than in the orthodox movement. Nature is experimenting lavishly; many of the species and individuals it produces show no survival value. In the same way, many of our attempts to find a solution will be abortive; but a movement which is petrified is an absurdity, a contradiction in itself. As long as it does not cope with changing situations and does not assimilate whatever valuable knowledge is available outside the temple, it will cease to remain a factor in the development of mankind. The psychotherapist who is scotomized with regard to semantics and gestalt psychology, to mention only two tools developed since Freud, will soon be out of date.

At present, my technique is based on function and experiment. What I will do next year, I cannot tell. Our aim is integration, and the analytical procedure is only one of many instruments toward this goal. I try to find out as much as possible about the patient's personality disorder by observation and discussion. Some dissociation or other is bound to become manifest in the first interview. Some anxiety, some talking around the subject will provide the opportunity to show him the existence of unrealized conflicts.

These conflicts have one pattern only: the identification-alienation pattern. This means: the patient identifies himself with many of his ideas, emotions and actions, but he says violently "No!" to others. Integration requires identification with all vital functions. Every attempt at integrating is bound to bring to the foreground some kind of resistance, and it is this bit of resistance I am after and not the content of the "unconscious." Every bit of re-sistance that is changed into personality as-sistance is a double gain as it sets free the jailer and the jailed.

I am fully aware that the patient cannot be immediately successful in the tasks which I put before him. If he could, he would not need my assistance. In this connection let us investigate the

From Planned Psychotherapy to Gestalt Therapy

basic Freudian experiment: the demand that the patient should say whatever is in his "mind." Actually no patient is free in his self expression. In an attempt to comply, he often gets the feeling that resistances are something bad, something that he should not have. He develops a technique of apparent compliance but keeps his statements on a dead verbal level. He talks around his resistances instead of about them; the barriers — embarrassment, fear, and disgust — which produce the dissociation are not experienced. The analysis is often kept on a level of unreality, for everything is related to a transference, that means to something that actually does not matter. The contact with the analyst is a blank; in it, interpersonal relations cannot be examined and discussed. Free associations, originally meant to clarify the meaning of a symptom, degenerate into a flight of ideas.

I can see no other way out of this dilemma than to start with the obvious, with the situation in which the patient finds himself during the interview. I suggest, for example, the following experiment: Let him begin every sentence with the words "here and now" and observe how he reacts to it. He may be co-operative or he may be a "slick customer" and begin a few sentences with "here and now" and then slip into yesterday and tomorrow at the first suitable occasion. Or he may be one of the obsessional types who attempt to make fools of other people. He might ridicule the experiment by saying, "Here and now on Friday I visited my friend." Another might ask, "What has this to do with my problems?" You can already appreciate from these few examples that the attitude of the patient is, as everywhere, also coming out in the session. Thus, if his character changes in his relation to the analyst it might also change in his other relationships. Already the first reactions give the analyst and the patient an opportunity to discuss some basic attitudes, the tendency to escape from the present, that is, from contact with reality, or the tendency to fool oneself and others (this is mostly not conscious) or the knack for plausible rationalizations.

Sentences like "Here and now" or "Now I am aware of" are chosen not only to bring out the top layer of the patient's character formation and some of the more primitive resistances but also to clear the path to the recognition of all his functions, especially, his dysfunctions, conflicts, attitudes of escape.

I have previously discussed the relativity of reality and its determination through the figure-background formation. When I use as synonyms, reality and actuality; when I stress the importance of "Here and now," I expect the Freudian to ask: "What about the past and the causes of the neuroses?" and the Adlerian to protest: "What about the future and the aims of our existence?" To these I must say: Unitary thinking does not recognize past, present, or future; it only recognizes processes to which we can artificially ascribe a beginning. If we like, we can call the beginning "cause" and the future event "purpose." Unitary thinking recognizes, how-ever, recordings of previous events and forms as precipitations of previous functions. It recognizes as aspects of the so-called future: planning, hope, predictability and vectors — but it maintains that these processes take place here and now. Moreover, a single sen-tence, even a word, is a time-space event. When reading a complex sentence, one may, as might be said, return to the past in order to pick up the lost thread, or as I would formulate it, consult quickly one's acoustic recordings to produce a meaningful *gestalt*.

Existence is actuality. It is awareness. For Freud, the present included the past 48 or so hours. For me, the present includes a childhood experience if it is vividly remembered now; it includes a noise on the street, an itch on my cheek, the concepts of Freud and poems of Rilke, and millions of more experiences whenever and to whatever degree they spring into existence, into my existence in the moment.

From Planned Psychotherapy to Gestalt Therapy

55

The initial difficulties in putting across the concept of functional thinking are sometimes considerable. Perhaps one can generalize and say: The toughest resistance is provided by what to the patient appears as obvious. To him it is obvious that one does not insult the analyst. It is obvious that one produces memories and, if possible, childhood memories. It is obvious that resistances are something undesirable, that one should not have them. It is obvious that one's difficulties have causes; that talking will bring the solution; that the therapist is either God or a fool.

Peculiarly enough, all great progress was made by examining the obvious. After taking over unsuccessful cases from other therapists, I have frequently discovered that the obvious had been taken for granted, not only by the patient, but by the therapist as well.

Here are several examples.

A man had had sixteen months of analysis. He liked his analyst and the analysis, but he had the impression that he had not made much progress. The obvious consisted in his case in the fact that the analysis meant for him lying on a couch and telling to the analyst all the unpleasant experiences of the previous few days. This obvious attitude was his means of preserving the status quo; namely, to bring up whatever he could not stomach. Instead of tackling any of the unpleasant experiences and profiting from them, he just "swallowed" them and "vomited" them out in his analytical sessions. He was not aware that he gulped down all his physical and mental food, but he was very much aware of a troubled stomach. He was not aware that he did not assimilate his experiences, but he knew that he had difficulty in understanding the world.

A lady who had considerable experience with psychotherapists put herself on the couch, lay stiff as a corpse, talked like an automaton and produced associations entirely irrelevant to her present life. She was dismayed to realize that I was not interested in the material she produced but only in how she produced it. Her previous analyst had not even noticed the obvious; namely, that this playing the corpse, this desensitization and immobilization was the center of her armor, of her resistance. The personality behind this armor showed a degree of disintegration approaching the psychotic border. I do not hesitate to make the classical technique responsible for this state of affairs. After six months of treatment she showed good recovery and a noticeable degree of integration.

A girl's obvious behavior was characterized by her continuous complaining about this or that person. She was full of complaints about her previous analyst. On my asking her what he had to say about these complaints, she answered that they were never discussed! And this happened with an analyst who believes in the transference mechanism! After having shown her that the complaining about someone to somebody else — for instance, about me to a friend instead of to his face was her way of avoiding aggressive contact, we proceeded to experiment with her attacking me. In this process a good deal of the previously unrealized fear and embarrassment came into the foreground.

A sculptor had derived satisfactory benefit from treatment by a progressive analyst; finally, it was decided to change analysts because two important symptoms stubbornly remained: his inability to work and his obsessional thought of killing his wife. After one of the first interviews I suggested that he should experiment with sculpturing the killing of his wife. The next day he returned enthusiastically, informing me that for the first time in years he had worked for three hours with interest and pleasure. His ability to express himself with pencil and clay, that is, on the nonverbal level, continued to be a great help in his treatment. The obvious that was overlooked in his case was that modeling, not language, was his means of expression.

In contrast to these cases there are those with whom I can achieve only little or no satisfactory integration. Apparently, they

From Planned Psychotherapy to Gestalt Therapy

take their customary outlook so much for granted that no other orientation seems feasible to them. In these cases I either lack the ability to show them convincingly the need for change and reorientation, or else myself am insufficiently integrated to be aware of the crucial resistance.

A psychologist was sent to me because she showed a number of characterological symptoms: among them was the desire to become a psychoanalyst. In spite of occasional emotional outbursts, there was no possibility of breaking through an armor of confused verbosity, a state which Landauer so beautifully called *faselige Verbloedung*. She refused to accept her need for personal treatment. We finally parted after she had decided that she could not afford a therapeutic analysis although she was willing to invest money to obtain the "easy and glamorous" life of a psychoanalyst.

At present, there are two more cases with me which look very doubtful. One is a paranoid man; the other is a near-schizoid young woman. The first's slogan for life is: "Rather to be important than healthy." The other is: "Rather to be clever and crazy than healthy and stupid." In both of these cases I have not been able to obtain satisfactory co-operation. Whatever experiment I suggest to the former, he proves to me that he can do it and leaves it at that. He behaves like a soldier who goes to war, shows his officer that he is able to hit the target and then thinks that he can go home. For him the war is over. What characterizes both cases more than anything else is their crippled spontaneity. Scheming and deliberate acting, blueprinting and preparing for all eventualities, in short, the futuristic thinking has become the obvious approach to life; thus contact with actuality has lost all meaning. Both are most of the time beside themselves and not within themselves. They are not "all there," in the true sense of the phrase.

Once one has worked through the basic character resistance, the battle is won. Not that the patient can achieve awareness en-

From Planned Psychotherapy to Gestalt Therapy

tirely on his own, but from that point on the increasing integration reverses the vicious circle of the neurosis. More and more, the "I" against "you" turns into a "we." Especially the second phase, the recognition of the motor tensions, of Reich's muscular armor, may evoke the patient's interest. Many a neurotic is given to hypochondriasis and other forms of introspection, and this phase of the treatment gives him plenty of opportunity for self-observation and, at the same time, a technique to cope with certain gross symptoms such as headache, backache, or anxiety states. Even should he apply the basically "wrong" method, that of relaxation, he experiences what appears to him miraculous results.

A lady continued with me after her former analyst had discontinued treatment because of her negativistic and aggressive attitude. She had originally started the analysis because of high blood pressure, a chronic pseudo-asthma, frigidity, and family difficulties. So great were her breathing difficulties when she started with me that she could scarcely speak. First, I decided to tackle her asthma and postpone work on the deeper personality disorder. After a few hours of reorganizing her breathing, she burst into tears of deepest despair, and with this she obtained her first relief. Three months later her asthma and high blood pressure had disappeared, and now after six months she has lost her frigidity. At present we are working on her self-consciousness. One experiment in particular brought home to her the mechanism of her armor. At a distance of about ten feet from me she was relatively at ease: upon coming nearer, she stiffened more and more and again lost the tenseness with distance. This reaction worked in an entirely automatic way. It was necessary to make her realize that *visualizing* the approach of somebody produced the same effect, and further, that she was not only stiffened but that she was also stifling something.

Besides Reich, there are a number of other schools that tackle the organism from the physiological functional aspect, or to speak

From Planned Psychotherapy to Gestalt Therapy

in dualistic language, which do body-analysis. They are, like the purely psychologistically-minded, condemned to the Sisyphus work of the never-ending unfinished situation. They have it, and they have it not. A certain amount of integration is possible; they are justified in their work because it is correct, but they do not realize the one-sidedness, the incompleteness, and therefore, the non-integrative nature of their work. Of course, they all claim, like many psychologically-or semantically-minded, that they deal with the organism-as-a-whole. All these movements, like the schools of F. M. Alexander, Elsa Gindler, and Jacobson of "you-must-relax" fame, will assist any kind of good psychotherapy. The greatest danger here is the same as with compartmental thinking and as with every non-comprehensive approach; namely, the avoidance of the crucial issue and the concentration on a dummy.

The person who shuns the solution of his sexual difficulties will often avoid the classical school. An analyst who unconsciously wants to exercise his lust for power will be careful not to assimilate the teaching of Adler or the Washington school. The man who does not want to face his inner conflicts will be attracted to one of the body-analytical schools. Thus, only a therapist with a comprehensive view will be in the position to spot and to tackle the central difficulties which the neurotic avoids facing.

Typical of the incomprehensive attitudes is the fetish of relaxation. Of course, a patient can go a long way in learning to relax, but he will become tense again in every situation where relaxation is not a figure, where he is confronted with some unwanted sensation, action, or emotion. It is not easy for our patients to learn that they are not required to relax deliberately but rather to become aware of the inner conflict of which the tension is only a part.

This brings us to the next step in integration. (As always, this subdivision into steps is artificial, and the different stages frequently overlap.) In this period the patient should get thoroughly ac-

From Planned Psychotherapy to Gestalt Therapy

quainted with the structure of his inner and outer conflicts and the acceptance/rejection concept. In the previous period he should have learned that a permanent stream of consciousness is going on, except in sleep or trance. He has become acquainted with a multitude of processes in the outer and inner world. In the present period we examine these processes in detail. Which ones are spontaneous? Which ones has he invented in order to comply with the analyst's expectation or his idea of treatment? Is his attention erratic or does he give the processes a chance to develop and become complete? How does he avoid following up the processes? Is he escaping into intellectualization, into facetiousness, into the past or the future, into listening to outside noises, sleepiness, monotonous speech, etc.? He is already aware of a certain amount of censoring and realizes primitive conflicts such as "This is embarrassing to tell," or "I should not think such things," "I want to relax, but can't," etc. The main difficulty lies in the fact that he mostly identifies himself with the censor. To him it is obvious that one should not criticize one's doctor, that people should have a good opinion of him, that it is permitted to hurt oneself but not others. However, by working through his muscular tensions, he is becoming much more aware of the structure of many conflicts; for instance, his efforts to suppress crying, anger, and so on.

The patient soon learns that the censoring is done by a very simple principle, by accepting and rejecting. He also learns by experiment to accept more of his drives and wishes. He realizes that by accepting and expressing his emotions he can get cathartic relief, and finally, that his ideas of accepting and rejecting are largely correlated to his pattern of orientation; namely, to his need for being accepted and his fear of being rejected by the world. He is astonished that in spite of his great need for approval; neither praise nor other tokens of acceptance have lasting effect but that refusals can worry and hurt for a long time. This apparent inconsistency results

From Planned Psychotherapy to Gestalt Therapy

from the characteristic neurotic tendency to leave many situations unfinished. If he learns to listen to the figure-background language of the organism and to act according to this reliable means of orientation; that is, to complete the unfinished situation, then he will be able to restore the balance of his personality and pave the way for productive development.

Let us take two simple examples of unfinished situations: one has the urge to urinate or one has an important letter to answer. One can reject the urge for a considerable time but the conflict between retaining and letting go will cost more energy than finishing the situation which would not take more than a few minutes. The same applies to the letter. The answer can lie on your conscience for days and weeks while the actual writing may cost you no more than an hour. Rarely will the situation finish itself merely by the passage of time and then usually not to your advantage.

Sleeplessness is a frequent symptom of unfinished situations; so are dreams. Probably the most important part of the dream is its end. Often the dream works toward the solution of a problem, but the dreamer cannot even stand the awareness during sleep and prefers to wake rather then finish the dream. Therefore, he wakes up before his wife gets smashed on the pavement since in the dream she has fallen out of the window, or before he enters the vagina in a lovemaking dream.

The next phase could be called *topological* re-orientation and reorganization of language.

Topological orientation is concerned with three processes, introjection, projection, and retroflection. In this paper these very interesting concepts can be treated only superficially. Each really requires several chapters. All three phenomena are symptoms of a lack of integration. In reference to introjection I disagree with Freud who recognized it as a pathological phenomenon only in total introjection and considered partial introjection to be a healthy process providing the building stones of the ego. My own contention is that every introject, be it partial or total, is a foreign body within the organism. Only complete destruction as preparation for assimilation will contribute to the maintenance and development of the organism. Destruction does not mean annihilating but rather the breaking down of the structure of physical or mental food. Freud said that it is not enough to bring material into consciousness, it must also be worked through. According to my analysis of the alimentary functions, I formulate this insight in this way: It is not enough to bring up undigested material; it also has to be rechewed so that the digestive process can be completed. This was true of the patient described earlier who annihilated the events he could not stomach by bringing them up in the consulting room. The cure involved resensitizing of the dead palate, becoming aware of the disgust barrier, remobilizing the clenched jaw, and investing his aggression in biting and chewing.

The topological aspect in regard to projection is obvious, but it requires special scrutiny. How is it that some part of a personality which should be experienced as belonging to the personal structure is disowned and treated as belonging to the outside world?

The child lives in confluence with its environment. It has not yet developed its contact functions. That is, it cannot differentiate between self-ness and other-ness, between subject and object, between projection and self-expression.

Confluence means the nonexistence or non-awareness of boundaries; means taking one-ness for granted. Confluence in the adult is sadomasochistic fixation, disguised as love. Hatred is frustrated greed for confluence; contact is appreciation of differences. Boundary means contact and separation: it means individuality.

If the state of confluence does not develop into the ability to make contact, or if by later desensitization the boundary is breached, then the infantile projection mechanism remains. Self-expression does not develop, as it presupposes the recognition and manipulation of the boundary. With this lack of adequate self-expression, an emotion will not be expressed and disposed of by emotional discharge, but it will be projected and remain in emotional connection with the personality. The personality becomes depleted and the projected properties cease to be useful instruments in the pursuit of personal aims. The paranoiac remains connected with his persecutor through hate, the religious person with his God through awe. Whether aggression, initiative, or responsibility is projected, in each case the result will be a crippled personality. Many neurotics project tendencies to accept and reject and thus cannot integrate these functions into discrimination. They remain connected with these projected tendencies by greed and fear.

The projection mechanism is connected with the linguistic problem. Through the projection of initiative and responsibility our patients experience themselves in a permanently passive role. A dream occurs to them. They are struck by a thought. Speculations go through their minds, brains, or whatever vacuum they choose for their perambulation. More specifically, this refers to the patient who is not willing to identify himself with his activities, who talks about his hard luck, about fate; who is the victim of circumstances. If his language is reorganized from an "it" language to an "I" language, considerable integration can be achieved with this single adjustment. One has to start this linguistic adjustment during the work on the muscular armor. Not before the patient fully realizes that there are not spasms in the small of his back, but that he is contracting, stifling feelings with the help of certain groups of muscles, can he develop or regain his ego functions and make contact with his muscular activity. Only then can he release tensions deliberately, for conscious control is indispensable for experimenting with whatever amount of rejected emotions or sensations he can tolerate and integrate.

From Planned Psychotherapy to Gestalt Therapy

The unity of linguistic and structural reorganization is equally essential in the treatment of retroflection. Retroflection is, one might say, the daily bread of the psychoanalyst. It coincides approximately with what Freud called "secondary narcissism." My objections against accepting this term are several. First, the so-called primary narcissism is not a pathological state. On the contrary, the lack of it, the lack of self-awareness, is detrimental to the personality. Second, retroflection or secondary narcissism has taken on a significance far beyond self-love, while in the customary language a narcissist remains a person in love with himself. Third, a descriptive term like "retroflection" is preferable to a purely symbolic one.

Retroflection is characterized by the word "self." Self-love, self-control, self-punishment, self-destruction, self-consciousness, and so on.

In retroflection one part of the personality is split from the other but it remains in active connection. Object relationship is replaced by an "I and Self" relation. In active retroflection, a tendency, e.g., love, destruction, control, scrutiny, etc. is directed toward one's own person. On the other hand, in passive retroflection, the "I" replaces the missing active object; I pity myself because nobody else does it; I punish myself in anticipation of someone else doing it to me.

Once the patient understands this mechanism he is on his way to recovery. Instead of being in a clinch, both parts turn toward the world; contact and expression are facilitated. Self-reproach will lead to depression and impotent resolutions, while object-reproach leads to object approach, to having it out, possibly to finishing a resentment situation.

In the projection mechanism, desensitization is apparent; in retroflection the malfunctioning of the motor system is more obvious. As a matter of fact, the good response to treatment is a result of the fact that the retroflective process can be easily demonstrated.

From Planned Psychotherapy to Gestalt Therapy

Whether the origin of the muscular suppression is the training in cleanliness or, as is more often the case, the hanging-on-bite, is immaterial. What is important is that a tremendous amount of motor energy is invested in the inhibition of catharsis and initiative. The muscular malcoordination is precipitated into symptoms which then constitute the manifest problem; clumsiness, constipation, asthma, headaches, etc.

Finally, we have to mention another set of powerful processes, the emotions. Just as the visible manifestations of processes in the human organism received the name "body," just as the awareness of the orientation/manipulation functions were called "mind," so the totality of the emotions was called "soul." This term tends to disappear in correlation to the progressive degeneration of our culture cycle in general and to the progressive emotional depletion of the neurotic individual in particular.

This depletion leaves the individual and society with ever greater unsureness, with the need to replace the biological means of orientation by intellectual ideas, by moralism, and by perfectionism. The pleasure-pain principle represents the biological compass whereby the organism finds its bearings, away from the painful and toward the pleasurable situation. Admittedly, a primitive compass, but one which is absolutely necessary for the individual's survival. What is good and bad for the individual coincides less and less with what society determines as good and bad, and still less with the neurotic's moralistic notions.

Integration, in the final analysis, is prevented by the desensitization of the emotional barriers, especially the disgust, embarrassment, shame, anxiety and fear barriers. Indifference is the best way of avoiding these experiences. Once these barriers come into existence, the patient still will avoid the complete situation, namely the conflict between self-realization and the interfering emotions. The negative emotions are indeed essential for the dichotomy of the personality. We have not only the task to expose them, but we also have to turn them into co-operative energies. During this process we encounter a transitory phase. Disgust turns via greed into discrimination; anxiety via excitement into specific interest, such as hostility, sexual excitement, enthusiasm, initiative, etc.; fear via suspicion into experimentation, that is, into widening the orbits of one's life; and embarrassment via exhibitionism into self-expression.

The treatment is finished when the patient has achieved the basic requirements: change in outlook, a technique of adequate self-expression and assimilation, and the ability to extend awareness to the nonverbal level. He has then reached that state of integration which facilitates its own development, and he can now be safely left to himself.

The changes which he experiences compare with his previous state in that he is now actually growing up while previously he tried to realize his infantile concept of an adult. Instead of taking his orientation from his desire to be accepted and his fear of being rejected, he is now doing the accepting and rejecting himself. Instead of living in oscillation between a jelly-like confluence with, and complete isolation from, his environment, he knows now that "contact" means acknowledgment of differences. Instead of experiencing himself as an outcast, he recognizes that he is a cell in the larger social organism, and that to be effective in this organism he must function to the best of his ability. He will integrate his interpersonal relations not by servile adjustment and sacrifice of his self-realization but by selecting contacts that make for a rich, productive existence.

Most of us realize that the science of personology is in its infancy and that much work has still to be done. The period of classical analysis is drawing to a close. In a few decades it will have a mere historical interest. The present period, which could be called

From Planned Psychotherapy to Gestalt Therapy

"the para-Freudian interval," started with the dissension of Alfred Adler. It is characterized by a multitude of promising reorientations, but also by a peculiar unsureness manifesting itself in a high degree of intolerance toward schools of different orientation. There must be a way to overcome this sterile isolation and mutual intolerance. There is a tie that can unite all of us: the frank acknowledgment that we know very little, that our orientation is as crude as the maps of the Phoenicians, that compared with other branches of knowledge we are beginners like Hippocrates or Paracelsus.

Have you ever been in despair when one of your patients had his vision blocked by his or your preconceived ideas, and didn't you wish then — to quote Freud — that he should display a more benevolent skepticism? I shall be very happy indeed if my paper has encouraged you to be benevolently skeptical toward both your own and my present convictions and to make the transition from any compulsive dogmatism to the experimental, insecure, but creative, pioneering attitude for which I can find no better example than the courage of Sigmund Freud.

From Planned Psychotherapy to Gestalt Therapy

The Theory of "The Removal of Inner Conflict"

Frederick S. Perls and Paul Goodman

Reprinted from Resistance, *Vol. 8, No. 4, March 1950*

Psychoanalysis has classically devoted itself to the uncovering of "inner conflicts" and their "removal." Certainly there is a world of truth in this concept, but even so we must inspect it much more closely than is usually the case. "Inner" presumably means either within the organism, inside the skin, or "within the psyche." For instance, a conflict between sexual tension and shrinking from pain, or between instinct and conscience. Opposed to these, and non-neurotic, would presumably be conflicts with the environment or with other persons. But put this way the distinction between "inner conflicts" and other conflicts is not valuable, for clearly there are non-"inner" conflicts that are profitably called neurotic. To the extent that a child has not yet grown freestanding from the child-parent field — is still suckling, learning to talk, economically dependent, etc. — it is pointless to speak of the neurotic disturbances

From Planned Psychotherapy to Gestalt Therapy

(unawares starvation, unawares hostility, unawares deprivation of contact) as either within the skin or within an individual's "psyche." The disturbances are in the *field*; they spring from the "inner conflicts" of the parents, and they result in the introjected conflicts in the later free-standing offspring, but their essence is in the disturbed felt-relation, irreducible to the parts. So the lapse of community in political societies is reducible neither to the neuroses of individuals (for indeed they become "individuals" because of the lapse), nor to the bad institutions (which are maintained by the citizens); it is a disease of the field. The distinction of "intra-personal" and "inter-personal" is a poor one, for all individual personality and organized society develop from functions of coherence that are essential to both person and society, such as nourishment, love, learning, communication, sympathy, identification; and indeed the contrary functions of division are also essential to both: rejection, hate, alienation, etc. Contact-and-boundary is prior to intra and inter, or to inner and outer. And disturbances that could be called neurotic occur also in the organism-natural-environment field, for instance the magic rituals of primitives that develop, quite without personal neurosis, from starvation and thunder-fear: or our contemporary disease of "mastery" of nature rather than healthy symbiosis, for quite apart from personal and social neuroses (which are, to be sure, here working overtime), there is a dislocation in the interaction of sheer material quantities and dearths, caused by unawares abuses. The primitive says, "The earth is starving, therefore we are starving," and we say, "We are starving, therefore let us wrest something from the earth"; symbiotically both are dreams.

In short, let us speak of "unawares conflicts" rather than "inner conflicts." This change is a fundamental simplification; for previously it was necessary to say, "we uncover the inner conflicts and bring them to the surface, make them awares," but now we can say "we make the unawares conflicts awares."

From Planned Psychotherapy to Gestalt Therapy

The classical wording, however, contains a very important truth, stated characteristically upside-down: namely that the inner conflicts, those inside the skin, within the organism — the opposed tensions and checks and balances of the physiological system — are for the most part reliable and not neurotic, they can be trusted to be self-regulating; they have proved themselves for thousands of years and have not much changed; they are not the subject of psychotherapy; when they are unawares they can be left unawares. It is, on the contrary, the meddling-inward of outside-the-skin social forces that deliberately upsets the spontaneous inner-system and calls for psychotherapy. These forces are new-comers and often ill-considered. Psychotherapy is, importantly, a process of disengaging these properly outside-the-skin forces from meddling inside the skin and disturbing organism-self-regulation. And by the same token, it is a process of disengaging such more distant unreliable economic and political forces, as competition, money, prestige, power, from meddling inside the primary personal system of love, grief, anger, parenthood, dependence and independence.

We come then to the terms "conflict" and "removal of conflict." Obviously in the classical formula "conflict" does not mean simply the opposition of tensions and the system of checks and balances that we have spoken of. The word is used pejoratively: conflict means "bad conflict," hence conflicts must be removed. Again let us distinguish carefully. The badness of conflicts seems, in the theories, to mean one or all of the following things: (1) all conflicts are bad because they waste energy and cause suffering; (2) all conflicts excite aggression and destruction, which are bad; (3) some conflicts are bad because one or both of the contestants are anti-social and, rather than let the conflict rage, the offender should be eliminated or sublimated, e.g. pre-genital sexuality or various aggressions; (4) false, mistaken, conflicts are bad. Now from our point of view, only the last of these propositions is unequivocally sound:

From Planned Psychotherapy to Gestalt Therapy

conflicts that are unreal, dummy, projected, displaced, etc. must be removed. But even in this case we must remember that behind every false conflict that is, where the contestants are erroneously conceived or are masks — there is a true conflict, of opposing real forces. The errors are tendentious, the masks express the real. Therefore we can say that, fundamentally, no conflicts should be removed by psychotherapy; but the goal of psychotherapy is to make awares unawares conflicts and to remove false conflicts. And indeed this may be simplified by omitting the last part, for once a false conflict is in awareness it dissolves of itself; one cannot be aware of what is not the case.

Here, on points (2) and (3) let us say only the following: where the contestants are natural drives they cannot be reduced, although they may be postponed by organism-self-regulation or even deliberately suppressed. When all the contestants are in awareness, a man may make his own hard decisions, he is not a patient; most often indeed, in such a case, a difficult drive spontaneously finds its measure by organism-self-regulation, without the need of deliberate choice.

Let us, then, consider conflict itself, awares and attended by suffering. The notion that conflict, whether social, interpersonal, or intrapsychic, is wasteful of energy, is plausible but superficial. Its plausibility is that if the work to be done could be got at directly, then it is wasteful for the contestant that will do the work to have to fight off an opponent; and perhaps both opponents can be made to join in as partners. But this is superficial, for it assumes that one knows beforehand what the work is that is to be done, and where energy is to be expended. Then the opponent must be deceived or he is lying. But where a conflict is real, *what* to do is just what is being tested. Even more, the true work to be done is perhaps *first being found out in the conflict; it was not hitherto known* to anybody and certainly not to the contestants. Surely this is true of any creative collaboration among persons: the best efficiency is attained not by establishing an a priori harmony among their interests and by their compromising their individual interests to a prearranged goal; rather, so long as they are in contact and are earnestly aiming at the best creative achievement, the more sharply they differ and have it out, the more likely they are to produce an idea better than any of them knew individually. It is the competition in games that makes the players surpass themselves. (We do not mean, of course, that *habitual* competitiveness is not a neurotic symptom.) In personal creation, also, as in art or theory, it is the warring of disparate elements that suddenly leaps to a creative solution. A poet does not reject an image that stubbornly but "accidentally" appears and mars his plan; rather he respects the intruder and suddenly discovers what his plan is, he discovers and creates himself.

The question is whether the same must not be true of intrapsychic emotional conflict. In ordinary healthy situations there is no problem: by organism-self-regulation a flexible instinct-dominance establishes itself, e.g. a strong thirst puts other drives in abeyance until it is satisfied. And longer range orderings healthily occur the same way: biting-chewing-drinking establish themselves over suckling, and the genitals establish themselves as the final aim in sexuality; genital orgasm is the conclusion of a sexual excitement. In the development of these orders there were conflicting tensions, but the conflicts worked themselves out. Now suppose the situation is unhealthy: e.g. the genital primacy was not strongly established because of oral unfinished situations, genital fears, so-called "regressions," and so forth. And suppose now that all these contestant drives are brought into the open, into open contact and open conflict, with regard to object-choices, behavior, interest. Must not this conflict and its attendant suffering and hardships be the means of coming to a self-creative solution, presumably the normal primacy? The conflict is severe because there is much to be destroyed.

From Planned Psychotherapy to Gestalt Therapy

Is the destructiveness to be inhibited? If this is the meaning of conflict, it is obviously unwise to allay it or to suppress some of the contestants, for the result must then be to prevent a thorough destruction and assimilation, and therefore to condemn the patient to a weak and never perfectly self-regulating solution.

From the physician's point of view, the danger in an emotional conflict is that its raging may destroy the patient, tear him to pieces. This is a true danger. But it must be met not by weakening the conflict but by strengthening the self and the self-awareness, so that as the conflict emerges and is attended to and sharpens, the self may sooner reach an attitude of creative indifference and identify with the coming solution.

From Planned Psychotherapy to Gestalt Therapy

Introduction to A Doctor's Report on Dianetics

From: A Doctor's Report on Dianetics: Theory and Therapy *by J. A. Winter. New York: Julian Press, 1951.*

At the time when psychoanalysis itself was commonly dismissed as a "crackpot" theory, I learned not to be intimidated by name calling. As one who has attempted to make contributions to psychoanalytic theory, I realize now, as I realized then, that the science of psychotherapy is not a closed or finished one. The division of psychotherapists into mutually hostile "schools" has been more destructive to the young science of psychotherapy than the earlier hostility of the layman; each school in its battle against the other has acted as if it had all the answers and, for the most part, has ignored insights of a rival school. Name-calling has become a substitute for independent thinking, the lifeblood of any science. The interests of this science (as well as of those who come to its practitioners for help) demand that I remain sensitive to the ideas

From Planned Psychotherapy to Gestalt Therapy

of others. Insights, even though badly or inadequately formulated, are worth investigating. The history of science is full of examples of valuable discoveries made by those who were not aware of their full, and often most important, significance.

While I am far from being a dianetician (it is not fear of what people might say that prevents me from being one), I have found that dianetics has suggested several new tools that have assisted me in my work with patients. Though the use that I make of these may be considerably at variance with the manner in which they were understood by Hubbard, I do not find it necessary to deny that his was the original idea, and my interest in the development of psychotherapy makes it important that I use this occasion to encourage the serious consideration by others of the significance and possible implications of dianetics.

Certainly, we must consider the provocative suggestion, intended or not, that the dianetic concept of the engram has given us relative to the concept of learning. This is a field which has been badly neglected in psychotherapeutic literature. Even where thorough studies have been made, as in dealing with backward children, the subject is largely confined to a study of inadequate orientation, inadequate semantic reactions and inadequate assimilation of reading material. For the most part, it is taken for granted that learning is a process of duration and repetition.

A very large area of learning, however, is characterized by suddenness, either by shock or (if such an expression may be permitted) by a pleasant shock; by what is called in Gestalt psychology the "Aha" experience. The burned child does not need any training to learn henceforth to avoid the hot stove, and the successful experimenting of the trial and error kind comes with a glow of success and insight of "That's it!"

"This will teach you a lesson" is an expression that shows how well aware we are of the connection of painful experience and learning. The avoidance of the painful, e.g., the punishment, becomes a powerful instrument in training.

In psychoanalytical literature this shock learning is called trauma, but it is conceived as a mechanical instance, as something that, unrelated to the human organism, descends upon it. The libido and death instinct theory leaves little room — except for "frustration" — for the meaning of the trauma. Dianetics, however, with its concept of engram, returns to the more realistic Darwinian theory of individual and race survival and gives trauma a more adequate meaning; at the same time, it supplements the inadequate psychoanalytic formulation of introjection.

In contrast to the otherwise hopelessly bombastic and mechanical terminology of dianetics, the term engram seems to be a good one. First, it merely means psycho-physical recording, leaving room for the possibility of beneficial shocks. Secondly, by linking up the survival significance of avoiding survival-threatening situations, it is a step towards a truly existentialist theory of psychotherapy.

Another way of learning is by copying, by imitation. If such copying is done unconsciously, psychoanalysis correctly regards this as a process of identification. But by assuming that all unconscious identification is introjection and by omitting the differentiation between identification with somebody's behavior (which is true learning; e.g., in the acquisition of a skill) and identification with somebody's command (which is not learning but submission) as well as by omitting the whole process of assimilation, the whole theory becomes confused. In addition, if the introjected object is, as Freud insists, a love object, then the introjective theory becomes cockeyed. Actually, we introject, we swallow, we avoid tasting and chewing that which we *dislike*, not what we love. Introjects and engrams are foreign bodies in the organism. Both have to be dis-

From Planned Psychotherapy to Gestalt Therapy

solved in order to be assimilated in such a way that they can contribute to the development of the personality.

To complicate matters still further, there is the joy that some children derive from obeying an adult's commands. This is a form of identification definitely not based upon introjection but rather upon *confluence*.

The essence of introjection is that something is swallowed that remains foreign material in the organism. As it is not assimilated, it can be recovered and redigested; this is an essential part of every successful therapy. Psychoanalysis has not overlooked instances of this sort, which it calls total introjection. A child has been through the painful experience of visiting a dentist; afterward, he plays at being a dentist with another child as the patient. Why? Because he loves the dentist? Certainly not! And introducing all kinds of auxiliary theories of transference and symbolic father actions in order to squeeze difficult facts into the libido theory is not very useful either.

Here again a piece of the dianetic survival outlook simplifies the theoretical concept. It says that we dramatize the *winning valence*; if we cannot do that, we become sick. Since in the fight for survival, the stronger has the better chance, and in the child's eyes the dentist is stronger than the patient, the identification tends to be with the party in power.

My observations over a long period of time are in accordance with this dianetic insight. The neurotic has a compulsion to vanquish at any price. This has often been recognized as the power drive; Adler and the post-Adlerians have emphasized this. What has not been considered sufficiently is the fact that the patient manipulates the therapist in such a way that he must get the better of him. This manipulation far surpasses in significance the importance of the transference mechanism. Whether he complies or resists, brings dreams that baffle or please; whether he wants to kill or efface himself — somehow he has to get the better of the therapist.

Taking into account this compulsive need for dominance, obsessional neuroses become easier to cure; they cease to be the bugbear of therapy. One has only to realize that both the *compelling* as well as the *compelled* part of the (equally) split personality want victory. The top-dog part does most of the manipulating by bullying, punishing, etc.; the underdog manipulates by empty promises, procrastination, forgetting, etc.

In the language of dianetics, both parts want to be in the winning valence, thereby bringing the internal war to a stalemate. Or, as Freud expressed it so beautifully, "If you have two servants quarreling, how much work can you expect to be done?" Only here there are no servants quarreling but rather the twin masters themselves.

There is nothing wrong with wanting success and victory, but there is everything wrong with the neurotic victory for the victory's and not for the benefit's sake. Despising the therapist, secretly making a fool of hint, rendering him impotent by being stupid, etc., are the favored tools, but such inadequate means don't help the patient to gain victories where he needs them: in his business, over his study material, in his games. Moreover, he has to learn that even without the victory his survival is not dependent upon getting sick, thereby manipulating some "ally" into taking care of him. Briefly, the neurotic does not have the antipoles *health* and *illness* or *victory* and *defeat* but rather a distorted dialectic: the alternatives of *victory* or *illness*.

The main difference between psychoanalysis and dianetics is this: the analyst works, for the most part, with interpretations; that is, with concepts, hoping that the thunderbolt of insight may strike home one day and make the patient realize that he is not a child any more, that his wife is not his mother. Dianetics, on the other

From Planned Psychotherapy to Gestalt Therapy

hand, relies (at least overtly) merely on experience, on perceptual awareness. Thus it has a better chance of rectifying *ad hoc* memories. Actually, dianetics has been as biased as Freudianism in its selection of the material to be processed. By expecting the patient to know Hubbard's book, an unprejudiced experience has been impossible, but the repeater technique, mainly the technique of contacting again and again all the perceptions and emotions, and above all (like Reich) the physical sensations, is of inestimable value. The patient *lives* his unfinished situations and does not merely "talk about" them. Thus he confronts his alter ego more effectively than in any other approach. Reich, if he had not been diverted by the compulsive search with microscope and telescope for the hypothetical, unrealistic "Libido" was on the way to developing a truly efficient mode of therapy.

The present book is not for anyone who has a fixation, a complete identification with any of the present day schools. A person with a fixation, as F. M. Alexander and John Dewey have pointed out, will experience everything strange as "wrong"; he will, as I described it, feel hostile to everything outside the ego-boundary. Hubbard, with his mixture of science and fiction, his bombastic way of pretending to something new by giving abstract names (Bouncer, Holder, etc.) to processes, his rejection of responsibility (only what has been done to you counts), his unsubstantiated claims, makes it easy for anyone to reject his work *in toto*, thereby missing any chance to extract any valuable contribution it might contain.

But is dianetics so basically different from the other psychotherapeutic schools? Don't they all, more or less, neglect or talk around the *Self*, its development and creativeness? Does not Freud consider only the intake (introjection) and output (catharsis) of the personality? Is not his Ego a poor something squashed between Superego and Id, the role of the self not even being mentioned? And do the more progressive schools deal with much more than the character, or at best, the Ego-concept rather than with the Ego-Functions? Don't they deal even less with the *semantic-integrative* functions of the self?

Likewise, the eclectic will have great difficulty in accepting what is valuable in dianetics. Not having assimilated what he studied, compartmentalizing rather than integrating the different approaches, he might have several fixations instead of one, and which again will prevent him from being unbiased.

Dianetics has swamped this continent and aroused enthusiasm seldom achieved by a book dealing with a psychiatric issue, but the straw-fire burned itself out just as quickly as it began. The discrepancy between claims and fulfillment was too great. And, as always, the revenge after a disappointment is that we forget any good we might have derived from the disappointer.

In this book, Dr. Winter has undertaken the task of salvaging what appears to be valuable in the dianetic effort. The modesty and honesty of the author is very impressive. He tries to come to grips with the essential problem: how can we account for the improvements and even cures that have been achieved with this particular therapy?

First of all, Dr. Winter gives us a detailed description of his technique and his opinions about its efficacy. He leaves open as unconfirmed whether the birth or prenatal experiences are genuine re-experiences, as claimed by Hubbard, or fantasies and projections as others insist.

He introduces the term of *multiordinality of the engram*. This is a valuable formulation, showing that a patient must be made aware of all the perceptual, abstract, symbolic and semantic aspects of a relevant phrase if it is to be effective therapeutically.

Most importantly, he introduces as the therapeutic agent the term of "differentiation," which refers to an act of rational decision

From Planned Psychotherapy to Gestalt Therapy

asserting that persons or actions were not what one had "believed" them to be. Thus with Dr. Winter, dianetics develops into a method whereby the irrational be it action or thinking (action substitute) is first experienced perceptually (along with its pain, obsolescence and insanity), then by an act of decision condemned as irrational (this is usually called insight). With this improved orientation a reorganization of one's actual behavior can be undertaken.

The author disassociates himself from Hubbard's "Everybody can heal Everybody"; he is well aware of the dangers involved in treatment by unskilled therapists. He knows that there are all too many neurotics who would treat others for the very same shortcomings for which they themselves need, but avoid, treatment.

Unfortunately, the author tends toward excessive speculation. These speculations stand in contrast to the otherwise careful appreciation of the new approach. They strike me as premature in part, although they seem valid in others. Furthermore, though Dr. Winter has assimilated much of Korzybski's outlook, he (like Freud and Reich) often mixes the *organism-as-a-whole* concept with obsolete concepts of the mechanistic mentality.

Notwithstanding these limitations, any psychotherapist, if he can overcome his fixation-bound scoffing (even if he only tries the repeater technique), will recognize in this book new tools for therapy. It is true that those who are hopelessly involved in a purely verbal existence will, again with words, "prove" that all this is nonsense. Or, as they usually formulate it: this is all old stuff; what isn't old stuff is wrong. But for the rest of you, read this book, try now and then a bit of the technique, but don't call it dianetics, for this would stigmatize you in the eyes of your confreres. If after a time you find something useful in this approach, remember that it was Dr. Winter who braved the storm of condemnation.

We need badly at present the recognition and assimilation of all therapeutic facts in our field; at the same time, we must avoid

From Planned Psychotherapy to Gestalt Therapy

the dangerous temptation to declare any one of them a panacea. This is true for dianetics as it is for the recovery of the Oedipus Complex, the stabilization of the self-system, the perfection of the orgasm, the dissolving of the character armor, the reorientation of semantic reactions, the reconciliation of animus and anima, the reconditioning of obsolete reflexes, the complete assimilation of introjects, etc. . . . all these aspects are valuable abstractions of the function of the human being within its environmental field. We have, however, to abstract; that is, to discover many more of these functions to achieve a comprehensive and reliable orientation. Then, and only then, shall we arrive at either a classification of neuroses and specific treatment, or, ideally, at a central theory which will unify facts and treatment without inconsistencies, compartmentalizations or blind-spots.

Frederick Perls, M.D., Ph.D.
Los Angeles, May 1951

From Planned Psychotherapy to Gestalt Therapy

Psychiatry in a New Key

"Psychiatry in a New Key" is a manuscript written by Perls sometime in the early 1950's, after the publication of Gestalt Therapy: Excitement and Growth in the Human Personality. *The title is a play on the title of another book, Susanne K. Langer's* Philosophy in a New Key: A Study in the Symbolism of Reason, Rite, and Art *(Harvard University Press; Cambridge: 1942, 1951). However, Perls changed the pun in his manuscript: Ms. Langer's "new key" is a reference to music; Perls' "new key" aims at opening the lock of all questioning procedures, both philosophical and psychological.*

Perls shows respect and admiration as well as a sincere questioning of Freud and his theories. Throughout "Psychiatry in a New Key" are indications of ideas that he integrated from the work of Kurt Goldstein, Alfred Korzybski, Andras Angyal, Lancelot Law Whyte and Alfred North Whitehead. (Interestingly, Langer's "Key" book is dedicated to Whitehead.)

Throughout the manuscript Perls is aiming at an understanding of how the organism/environment field approach could became a unified field theory for all of the psychological sciences. "Our intention is . . . to debunk another ill-fitting key, the concept of our 'having' a mind, and to try out a no-mind approach." He wanted to use Gestalt theory to develop a more rigorous, complete picture: a descriptive language of human behavior and misbehavior.

Again, Perls does not use "Gestalt therapy" to identify his thinking.

From Planned Psychotherapy to Gestalt Therapy

★   ★   ★   ★

Lock and key are mutually dependent. Change the lock and we shall have to change the key. If the key at our disposal does not open the door, it could well be that we have lost the right key. If we continue in our endeavor to open a door with a key that will not easily unlock it, we certainly do not behave quite sanely. It would be quite rational, however, to try a new key. It is the aim of this book to forge this new key by using the method of debunking. This method consists of re-examining a question rather than answering the question as it stands. If the recast results in unmasking the question as phony, we have to reformulate the whole problem as such.

An instance in question is the problem: "What comes first, the chicken or the egg?" Since the chicken-egg-chicken-egg-chicken-egg, etc., sequence is a process that goes on for thousands of years, we can answer our question only by reducing the abstract problem to a concrete one and determining which egg precedes which chicken. Some centuries ago a similar distinction between concrete and abstract succeeded, for some people at least, in reducing to absurdity the argument as to how many angels could dance on the point of a needle.

As far as psychiatry is concerned, the first great step was taken after debunking the principle that the soul was made from different stuff than the body and that it could leave and return to its abode. Here, indeed, was a key which could unlock many secret doors of the human organization. Our intention is, similarly, to debunk another ill-fitting key, the concept of our "having" a mind, and to try out a no-mind approach.

Certainly, many great thinkers have been, and still are, busy solving the mystery of mind and body. Many important discoveries have been made and many excellent theories have been brought

From Planned Psychotherapy to Gestalt Therapy

forward, but, as the cat always falls on its feet, they always come back to the mind as if it were something that existed somewhat isolated from the body. True enough, on purely theoretical grounds, they will defend the thesis of an organismic unity or of a psychosomatic oneness. Often they will fall back on another split: Consciousness versus the Unconscious; or they postulate a psychological cause for a somatic event (or vice versa). But once it comes to debating, then they have "thoughts" in their "minds." Consequently, we have not yet achieved a true and consistent concept of the human being as a coherent whole, although we already have some sound theories about it. The names of Whitehead, Goldstein, Angyal, Whyte and Korzybski will bear this out.

How is it, then, that all these keys do not open the door to the so much needed theoretical simplicity which alone can lead to a full understanding of human behavior (and misbehavior)?

In my opinion, the fault lies in neglecting to examine the obvious. To wonder about events which everybody takes for granted is always the Source of new viewpoints, discoveries and inventions. The obvious, in our case, lies in our use of language. We take for granted that we think up or use existing words and are *a priori* convinced of their sense. Since we use these words, we are convinced that we have a consciousness and that we have a mind. The richness of their connotation has prevented us from examining their denotation.

Let us do this now and see whether or not these terms are good keys. I believe they are not. I believe they are — hybrids — as if we were to dream up a "Horsemobile," which would have the functions and properties of a living animal and a mechanical vehicle at the same time.

There were times when people took the existence of ghosts for an actuality, and children still do. Now just imagine that we took the Horsemobile as a reality and fed him hay when he needed

From Planned Psychotherapy to Gestalt Therapy

gasoline, or expected him to do ten miles per hour and could not believe that he would do seventy miles per hour. Or we might start arguments in learned societies as to whether he were an animal or a machine, or discuss his Mind and Unconscious (or perhaps he has none). However we look at him, if we believe in him, he will be the source of utter confusion to himself, to the owner and to the world.

It's hard to believe that "mind" and "consciousness" are just such Horsemobiles. We could call them *Fantattention* and *Will-aware*: hybrids of Fantasy and Attention — which we now denote Mind — and of deliberate Willing and Awareness — now spoken of as Consciousness. "Now you see it, now you don't!" Our hybrids can make themselves invisible, become real *Paltergeister* or even *dei ex machina*. As such, they are called the Unconscious.

What would happen if we did not fall into these verbal traps? What would happen if we deprived these hybrids of their power? What is their power? Under the mask of helping us to understand ourselves, they merely contribute further confusion, as though we had not enough areas of confusion to deal with as it is. As Goethe said, "Just strive to confuse your audience; it is hard to satisfy them."

The advantage that will accrue from re-examining "mind" and "consciousness" is that it will get us out of the blind alley in which we now find ourselves. It will, as I hope to show, cast new light as to the nature of the Ego and prepare the way for a unified-field theory that is consistent, coherent and applicable.

As suggested before, "mind" has at least the two meanings of attention ("I put my mind to it") and of fantasy ("I saw it in my mind's eye"). The use of mind as another term for attention provides no difficulty, but we have need of a mare extensive discussion about the connotation of fantasy.

From Planned Psychotherapy to Gestalt Therapy

When Freud set out to debunk the then current opinion that Consciousness or the Ego (both terms are fairly synonymous for him) was the master in its home and was the ruling agency of the personality, he was undoubtedly referring to the equation of Consciousness = Deliberateness. Will-power was the prerequisite for self-control, and the conscious mind or the "I," was endowed with the ability to exercise it. But by increasing the other side of Consciousness, the awareness (as he set out to do), we improve our orientation, but we don't increase the will-power. By decreasing deliberateness we increase spontaneity, we diminish self-control, which is all to the good.

What we have to do is to abandon the confusing terms of Mind and Consciousness and be satisfied to operate with the cleaner terms of attention, fantasy, awareness and deliberateness.

The psychologist or psychiatrist may mourn the loss of two of the apparently most important words of his language, but he will grieve still more if we consequently leave the Unconscious to the same fate. If this be a consolation, we use the word "unaware," but give it a much wider scope than what was designated by Freud as the unconscious. The latter is identical with the Repressed, that is, with the once conscious material. Freud compares the Conscious and the Unconscious with an iceberg. Rather, we compare aware and unaware with the surface of the globe, and say that what we don't see must not necessarily have been on the surface before. In other words, we say that what we are unaware of now might have been in awareness before, but that there is much more which never has come into awareness or which has faded or been assimilated or built into larger Gestalten, such as many skills or patterns of behavior. We also might call it the unknown or even the unknowable.

Generally, the trend in language is from the literary to the more and more abstract and symbolic meaning. For instance, if I call someone a bastard, I am not insinuating that he is an illegiti-

From Planned Psychotherapy to Gestalt Therapy

mate offspring. I use that term to hurt him by classifying him as something despicable. Not so with the bastard-words (note the return to the original meaning): Consciousness and Mind. Rather than remaining the abstract terms which they are, they have been concretized; they have assumed the meaning of actual objects, mainly of geographical places in which certain events take place. This has been carried to such a degree that Freud unashamedly speaks of a topological orientation, a notion not less absurd than angels dancing on needle points.

All of us have upon occasion had experiences which make us feel hellish or heavenly. But we do not pretend to concretize these feelings and are certainly not convinced that, at those moments, we are in places where real devils torture and angels sing cantatas. If we do, we either admit to fantasizing or we project these images into the post-mortal future.

"I have a notion in the back of my mind;" "my mind was teeming with ideas;" "there is nothing in my consciousness;" "I have an Oedipus complex in my Unconscious"—in all these expressions Mind and Consciousness apparently have body and substance, and the thoughts and dreams do all kinds of things within that body, with peculiar traffic regulations between the conscious and unconscious thrown in. The mind/body dichotomy is not solved by making the mind a bodily container of the "mental;" it is merely further obfuscated. The soul/body dichotomy has returned, though admittedly in a very modified form.

We are not engaging in idle philosophical speculations, for these fantasies (called concepts) about the concrete mind are precisely the reason why the genius of Freud has failed and why psychoanalysis so often is bound to fail. As long as repression is considered the only method of disowning one's thinking and feeling, while other means of dissociating the mental and the physical are maintained, no true integration of the personality can take place.

From Planned Psychotherapy to Gestalt Therapy

The Mind and Consciousness concepts are precisely the means whereby the dissociation survives in most cases all the prolonged efforts of psychotherapists of nearly all denominations.

How much better off are we if we replace Mind by fantasy? Are we perhaps generalizing and taking a genus for the species? Isn't fantasy one of several domains of Mind? Is it not on a par with reasoning, remembering, dreaming, and other activities of the mind?

Admittedly, there is a difficulty here. The connotation of fantasy is that of imaginary, unreal, not being identical with a true copy of the actual world. On the other hand, fantasy also has the aspect of novelty, of uniqueness, of creativeness. This, too, is not specific for fantasy. Any true contact of the individual with the world has the character of novelty, if it is experienced. This is so much the case that we can describe human development as a continuous transformation of novelty into routine.

The method of defining and pigeonholing seems to get us nowhere. So let us try and start from simple observations. I see a tree. To do that I need the eye and the registering brain. I have to direct my attention or pay attention to it; then I become aware of something that I can recognize and, if I wish, label "tree." I then shut out the environment, close my eyes, or stare into the blue. I visualize a tree. We easily could say that I imagine a tree. This can, but may not be, the exact replica of the previous tree; in any case it is an actuality, but not a physical reality, of which I am aware. I imagine "looking" at a tree. This is important because it is not the tree which is relevant in this case, but the fantasized activity of looking.

Furthermore, very little introspection will suffice to convince one that most of what one calls thinking is fantasizing of "talking to some person known, unknown, or to oneself." There is no second

From Planned Psychotherapy to Gestalt Therapy

nose to smell with, no third ear to hear with, once we are engaged in these imagined activities.

The purpose of these fantasy activities is to provide a substitute for the physical activities which they represent. Freud called the activity of the mind *probe handlung* — "acts of trying," which is a brilliant observation. The task of fantasizing, especially of rational fantasizing, is indeed to restrict our physical activities up to the point where they appear as homeopathic or diminutive actions.

The advantages of "acting in effigy" are manifold. A great amount of time and energy is saved, as typified by even the crudest examples of planning or shopping. Instead of physically going to place after place, store after store, you imagine the activity and the contents of the store, and narrow down your choice. Suppose you hesitate in the choice of the right word or its spelling. You don't run to the dictionary or thesaurus every time; often it will be sufficient to search your word reserve for the correct answer. Or if you have mislaid something, it is frequently more efficient to search for it in fantasy than motorically.

Look at those expressions which we use to describe our fantasy-life: "we grasp an idea;" "we grope for a word;" "we search for a memory." We don't move our hands, except perhaps for a gesture. This process is known as fading; Metaphors lose their original literary meaning and assume more and more symbolic connotations. The clasping of the hand, which once was a ceremony of non-aggression, is in Europe reduced to a trivial everyday gesture; so is the kissing of the hand, once a sign of deep devotion. "Gentleman" was previously a title of distinction. Today the inscription on a lavatory door tells you that you are one.

Children don't think first and then talk. The whole process is a very complicated one which involves sub-vocal talking, formulating and verbalizing. Children first form sounds, play with sounds and soon with words. Later they learn to whisper and to conceal their speech by fantasizing their speaking ("children should be seen, but not heard"), by making the vocal "sub"-vocal.

A similar process takes place with a good memory. If we disregard the vague, often purely verbal, recall, we realize that in any experienced moment of the past we actually transport ourselves to the place and time of the event, as though we had a fantastic time/space machine at our disposal. But note: we do not and cannot go back into the past in physical actuality. The whole process is taking place here and now and in imagination only. The same holds true with our futuristic thinking, be it planning or daydreaming. All attempts to predict and thus annihilate the future are taking place here and now in our, or our teacup reader's, fantasy.

It is paradoxical that Freud, who was so preoccupied with the past, should have coined the term of *probe-handlung,* because the purpose of such rehearsing in fantasy is precisely "futuristic thinking," e.g., preparing for the moment of committing oneself to speech or other physical action. The greater the dread of the unknown of the future, the more intense is the safeguarding and preparing in physical actuality as well as in one's fantasy life.

At this point, we need not say much about psychopathology. The discrepancy between the neurotic's imagination and the physical actuality has always been assumed to be the essential symptom. Seldom, for instance, are the laws of a country even half as stern and vindictive as the Super-ego of a melancholic or obsessional character.

If I say to a touchy person, *"Maroube,"* he will react with curiosity. If I say, "You son-of-a-bitch," he will claim that he feels hurt, without having received any physical injury whatsoever. (But of course he feels hostile; he wants to hurt; he first projects his need to hurt onto me.) Proof? He could not localize the hurt in any part of his body, but he feels "as if" I had slapped him, that is, he imagines a physical assault.

From Planned Psychotherapy to Gestalt Therapy

In a paranoiac or paranoid character there is the inability to discriminate between observation and the projection of his imagination. He has suppressed his own fantasies of attack, injuring and pursuing, has externalized those fantasies and made himself the abject "hurt" from the outside.

Let us now return to the saner occupation of rational thinking. Is this also "merely" a product of our fantasy? I believe that this is so to a great degree. Thinking is essentially the manipulation of symbols, be it numbers, words or other symbols. Here, too, the transition from physical actuality to fantasizing can easily be traced. For example, it is characteristic of the genius that he can make complicated manipulations or calculations in his fantasy where others have to do the work with paper and pencil in a physical actuality.

We could continue *ad infinitum*. We could talk about the self-concept, that imagined ideal one wants to achieve; we could discuss those fantasies we make up about what the world is like, fantasies which we call hypotheses or theories and which actually are miniature models or maps; we could consider the religions of the aborigines and other *weltanschauungen*, and we would discover that all these are fantasies designed to approximate physical reality.

What have we proved and how can our approach lead us to a unitary concept of the human? We can progress toward this concept by applying the dialectical law that changes of quantity or degree can produce changes in quality. This can also be said of intensity. A difference in degree of temperature changes the quality of ice into that of water. And with a differing degree of intensity, physical behavior changes into mental behavior. For want of a better label and in order to make a break with the dangerous use of the word "mind," we call this mental behavior "fantasy" — rational or irrational (for physical behavior, too, can be rational or not); Our formulation is now that the human organism acts upon and reacts to the environment in greater or lesser intensity. Overt behavior changes into latent, private activity.

The diminished intensity is of tremendous advantage for the development of human beings. The saving of energy otherwise consumed by "acting out" can now be invested in enriching the possibilities and choices. But the development does not stop here. The ability to abstract and to combine abstractions, the capacity for inventing tools and symbols, the creation of art and science, further demonstrate that the ability to fantasize made possible the great step from the animal to the human.

The origin of fantasy lies in frustration. If there is satisfaction, the Gestalt is closed and no excitement is left for continuing the event in question. The daydream and often the dream, which are ersatz satisfactions and denials of frustrations, bear this out. To understand the relation of fantasy and frustration we have to turn to the other content of "mind"; we have to examine the nature of "attention." Such investigations will bear out something else, namely, the recognition that we need integrative concepts like the one demonstrated above.

Any living organism shows two all-important tendencies: to survive as species and, as an individual, to grow.

Let us oversimplify the situation and postpone the discussion on growth. Let us further assume that we have shown that the human being is an organism with many abilities, such as breathing, digesting, feeling, moving, using its senses and acting in minute quantities, that is, fantasizing, etc. As it is not a mechanical thing, the organism uses up much of its substance in the process of living, and this has to be replaced. We speak of homeostasis as the term indicating the precious balance in which the optimum of well-being is maintained.

Such an optimum means: neither too much nor too little. A lack of water leads to dehydration, a surplus to edema, a lack of

From Planned Psychotherapy to Gestalt Therapy

thyroid to mongolism, a surplus to Basedow's disease. The organism is so "organized" that it tends to replenish the lack and shed the surplus in order to maintain the required balance. We correctly speak of a balanced diet to point to the need for proteins, fats, carbohydrates and vitamins. What holds good for the diet applies to every need. We conclude that it is too arbitrary to confine human needs to an enumeration of instincts, be it the Freudian Eros and Thanatos or the McDougall fourteen. Any constellation in which the organismic balance is upset produces the urge to restore it. Thus, we do not assume that an instinct is something situated somewhere in the organism like a gland. If we could classify all the disturbances of the organismic balance, we probably would find many thousands of instincts, and even these in themselves differ in intensity.

Let us exemplify this in a simple organismic event: the loss of water. Physiologically, we call this dehydration; sensorically, thirst, with its symptoms and restlessness; psychologically, wish to drink; chemically, loss of x units of H20.

Now no organism is self-sufficient. It is situated in an environmental field. As a matter of fact, we consider the relatedness of the organism to its field the essence of psychology. Not the study of the organism — this is a matter of anatomy and physiology; not the study of the environment—this belongs to the physical, geographical and social sciences—but the relatedness of the organism to its field. Harry Stack Sullivan has covered a large part of it under the name of "Interpersonal Relations," and Freud made a great contribution with his notion of cathexis.

*   *   *   *

The concept of cathexis or *Beasetzung* (occupation, possession) was a new light illumining much of the relatedness of the organism's instincts with its environment. It rectified an error which biology had introduced: the theory of the reflex arc, a semi-mechanical concept which biology cherished and still clings to.

The persistent basic philosophical question whether man is ruled by forces from without or within is once more confusing us. As is so often the case, the "either-or" approach, the need for a simple causality, the neglect of appreciation of the total field, makes problems and decisions out of situations which are essentially indivisible but in which the introduction of any split is artificial. Such an example was discussed above in relation to the mind/body split.

The split concerning us here is based on the fallacy that the inside/outside experience consists of two parts. True enough, on the verbal level I can divide the sentence, "I see a tree," into an act of seeing and an object. However, in actuality the process of seeing cannot possibly exist without something that is seen. Likewise, hearing or any other sensing makes no "sense" if there is nothing to be sensed; However, if I see a tree, I might equally well exclaim, "A tree!" thereby bracketing off the seeing and accenting the external object, the tree; In that case, I take the sensing for granted and I shall refer to it only when its absence becomes apparent: "Don't you see? Are you blind?" I can also shift the emphasis on the process of sensing by using slightly different terms: "I look at, or for, the tree," or "I listen to the whistle;" Obviously, these vocables indicate a greater participation from my side and do not take for granted that the objects automatically send their light rays or sound waves mechanically into my system, as the reflex arc theory would have it.

If such a theory were correct, if the receptors were open for whatever rays are there to excite them, then we would only mirror the chaos of the millions of colors, shapes and so on which confront us simultaneously;

From Planned Psychotherapy to Gestalt Therapy

The situation changes completely if we reverse the established order, which reads: first receptor, then intermediate system, then effector, into one which sees a central agency with two branches connecting us with the world: the sensoric and the motoric systems. As anatomical terms these are nothing new; we call their psychological equivalents the systems of orientation and manipulation. (We use these terms as abbreviations for the execution of acts. Unfortunately, manipulation has for many people some unsavory tinge, but we mean to apply it without moral evaluation, likening it to the manipulation of the keys of a piano.) The principle that the organism reaches with both systems towards the world gives us another step towards the concept of the organism coping with the world."

For the experimental proof of this new orientation, the reader is referred to the work of Kurt Goldstein and other modern neurologists. However, for practical purposes let us acknowledge that the low order reflexes, such as the patellar and the iris, will keep their places, as the gas stove keeps its own, in spite of the thermodynamic theories in modern physics.

With the new outlook, the environment becomes a function of the organism rather than its victim; the organism selects actively what it needs, rather than reacts mechanically to the world. Objects of the world receive, as Freud puts it, a cathexis. This means something is going on between the organism and certain objects. The Latin word for this is interest; the Gestalt terms are that some foreground figure stands out against a background.

When we deal here with the *relatedness* of the organism and its field we are, so far, thinking (imagining) a situation with no mind (fantasy). We are not yet dealing with the sophisticated citizen of the modern world. We are dealing, so to speak, with the centipede before he becomes confused when asked which leg he moves first.

From Planned Psychotherapy to Gestalt Therapy

Such a question obviously interferes with his moving, as a unit, within his field toward his food, which had received a cathexis, aroused his interest, stood out against the indifferent background of soil.

The relatedness of the organism to its field is exactly that of a dialectical opposite. To achieve the homeostasis the organism has to find its required supplements in the environment. The system of orientation discovers what we want. We sense the satisfying stuff; we look for what we need (without intellectual knowledge, without visualizing, imagining) directly. Instead of coping with the millions of shapes and forms and noises, we merely go for whatever becomes foreground figure. Think of a mother who sleeps through the loudest street noises, but is awakened by a slight whimpering of her baby.

Once the orientation has done its job, we still have to manipulate the cathected object in such a way that we can achieve the organismic balance, that we can close the Gestalt in question. The mother will not be satisfied with merely hearing her baby whimper; she will do something in order to eliminate the source of disturbance. In the best case she will satisfy the acute need of the baby, and with its satisfaction achieved, she, too, can resume her sleep.

*   *   *   *   *

We have previously assumed that there ore thousands of instincts, thousands of constellations which can unbalance the organism. If they all simultaneously produced a cathexis, we would be confronted with a confusion no less than if there were no facilitation of orientation. We would be driven to do too many things at once.

From Planned Psychotherapy to Gestalt Therapy

Perhaps you have wandered why science and we, in general, are so keen on unified concepts, on integrative ideas.

If our attention is only divided between two objects of interest, we already experience "lack of concentration," a frequent complaint of the neurotic. If there are more, or if the object of "concernful interest" is hazy, we feel confusion. If there are two incompatible situations requiring our attention, we speak of conflict. If these are persistent and apparently insoluble, we regard them as neurotic conflicts.

We must assume, therefore, that there is more involved in the relation of the instincts and their objects of satisfaction than merely cathexis. We have to presuppose that there is an organismic self-regulation which tends to prevent the appearance of more than one attention-demanding item at a time. We must presuppose such a selective operation, for we see that the organism can effectively deal only with one thing at a time, that we can focus on only one object clearly.

This kind of organization is advantageous for survival from two points of view: the organism can always, if required, concentrate all its faculties towards the focus of attention, and it can deal with first things first.

The benefit that results from concentrating all one's abilities, the clearness of orientation, the freedom of choice, the mobilization of one's skills, hardly needs to be stressed. Yet in our civilization of safety we are so seldom confronted with emergency situations that the survival value of this kind of concentration has become rather dim. People who live in full security and without even neurotic dreads are likely to feel that their lives are empty and dull. However, some manage to introduce artificial stimulation (gambling, racing, etc.), which produces some need for concentration.

From Planned Psychotherapy to Gestalt Therapy

★   ★   ★   ★   ★

Greater difficulty is provided by the other problem: first things first. We cannot assume that we have an instinct in ourselves that makes deliberate decisions as to the sequence of actions. This ability to organize ourselves according to plans is a very late acquisition. The organism, in order to survive, must do this kind of regulation instinctively.

In Africa I have observed deer grazing within a hundred yards of sleeping lions. When a lion awoke and uttered its hunger sound, however, they took speedy flight. Here is a model for all autonomous instinct regulation. We have a hierarchy of instincts in order of their survival value. Could we form a fantasy (hypothesis) of how this kind of selectivity might take place?

We could, for instance, imagine ourselves in the deer's place. Suppose we were running for our lives. Such extreme situations produce tremendous excitement, an excitement that would work itself off by the run. We might soon run out of breath; in this case, we would have to slow down or stop altogether until we got a second wind. In other words, breathing would become a greater emergency than running, just as running previously became more important than eating. We do not have to stop and decide that we need a breath. The organism automatically attends to the most urgent life-supporting function. To run well, we need the support of good muscles, coordination, increased output of energy. This means increased metabolism, burning up of stuff that produces the energy. Burning is oxidizing. The material to be oxidized (carbohydrates, etc.) is stored in the organism, but the oxygen is not stored; it is inhaled as the situation demands it. This is why breathing plays such an enormous part in all situations of increased activity, especially in increased motoric and emotional activity.

From Planned Psychotherapy to Gestalt Therapy

101

About the relation of breathing to anxiety we shall talk in another context. Here I merely want to point to the relation of breathing to excitement and indicate that in an integrative theory one might call the basic psychological energy "excitement" as equivalent to the physiological term "excitation." Again let me emphasize something mentioned in connection with "manipulation." No evaluation is meant. Some people see in excitement something valuable; some reserve it for some forms of excitement and exclude others. "Now don't get excited." "Oh, it was so exciting!" These two phrases alone show the inconsistency of our approach to excitement as something desirable or the contrary.

"Excitement" is a more general term than Freud's "libido"; "excitement" is also more concrete; it can be felt specifically and leaves open the kind of excitement which is experienced, from the hazy feeling of "nervousness" to the clearly perceived fury. Bergson's *elan vital* is close to this meaning, but it still has, at least for me, same sense of a dichotomy, as if a body were contrasted with an energy, as if somehow the body and the elan vital were two different kinds of "stuff." Furthermore, as will be seen, taking excitement as the base, we can arrive at a consistent theory of emotion.

In spite of Freud's brilliant and precise formulations, we find a number of areas of confusion. So with the relation of libido and emotions. On the one hand, according to Freud, affection "is" libido; on the other, grief "liberates" libido, not to speak of all the other functions which are attributed to libido. At best, libido is a part of a dualistic *weltanschauung*, of the struggle between Eros and Thanatos.

But we have seen that the organism can cope only with one thing at a time. Thus, an integrative orientation, as long as it is coherent, will save much confusion. The primitive polytheistic myths and religions seem to contradict this, and only the notion of

From Planned Psychotherapy to Gestalt Therapy

the abstract X, the unspeakable, the not concrete (for instance, the God of Moses) seems to provide such on integrative concept. But, as Cassirer has shown, the primitive experiences life and himself in it as a coherent oneness. In our time we have such an integrative concept again, at least as far as the inanimate universe goes, in Einstein's unified-field theory. No one will deny that this facilitates the orientation within the universe and its "energies." Likewise, we need for individual psychology a unified-field approach, in which time, space, mass, energy and behavior appear as mere abstractions of a central concept: the organism embedded in his surroundings. Our school hopes to make its contributions toward this goal mainly by eliminating splits such as psychology and psychopathology and other dichotomies, which were discussed in previous publications.

So far we have treated homeostasis as a semi-static concept. We have seen that there are many instinct circuits which originate through on imbalance of the organismic substance. The organism "needs" something. The needs are, as supplements, perceived in the environs, and the organism sets out to cope with such needs. We also saw that according to our organization we can cope best with one situation at a time, that there is a precedence of the more life-supporting need over the lesser. This means that the less important ones have, so to speak, to wait. Again with his uncanny intuition, Freud dimly realized this, and, as a projection, called this delaying tendency the reality principle.

To form a picture of how in our fantasy (hypothesis) this kind of figure-background principle works, we have first to make a step toward "thinking in processes." It is convenient, as psychoanalysis does, to think of instincts or complexes as "things" that can be repressed or transported from one locality to another. But actually there are so many processes grossly and subtly going on all the time, forming together an atmosphere or mood, that again we would lapse into utter confusion, if it were not for the preferential

From Planned Psychotherapy to Gestalt Therapy

treatment of the uppermost needs. These contain enough excitement to get into the foreground, with many more unsatisfied needs — nay, in the human, with many more "unfinished situations" — waiting for the foreground to be emptied, in order to obtain the closure of their Gestalt, that is, to achieve satisfaction. Thus, with satisfaction, both the need and the cathected object disappear from the foreground. This, in a nearly mathematical way, becomes obvious in the example of thirst, where the exact number of units of fluids the organism requires can be measured. The same amount added to it from the environment will add up to zero. Or if, without any deeper involvement, a man's interest is centered around sexual gratification only, he will, after completed orgasm, look at his watch. Any affection demanded from him *post festum* will be a bother, i.e., receive a negative cathexis; he will dread it.

Man is suspended between impatience and dread. Each need requires immediate gratification without any lapse of time. Impatience is, thus, in the presence of frustration, the emotional form which excitement assumes first. Dread is the basis of all negative cathexis; it is the anti-survival experience. If the immediate gratification is not forthcoming, the organism will increase its excitement, which is then experienced as anger. "I am impatient with you," shows already the tinge, sometimes the clear color, of anger.

If all the needs have this impatience, how can the organism achieve the dominance of the most urgent?

If during a "talky-talky" party (phrase from Paul Goodman) a lot of verbal noise fills the room and I want to understand what somebody says in the other corner, because I became interested in the intensity of his gestures, I might hush the other talkers. As it is, his words don't stand out against the general noise. They can stand out in clearer relief only by contrast. He either will have to raise his voice, or the general noise has to be subdued. If I am not successful the first time, I will increase my energy, became more impatient or angry.

Something similar is done in radio. If the required station is tuned in, the hissing of the background is subdued; the contrast of the foreground music to a background of complete silence is what is desired.

The subduing of the background can go up to the point of its complete annihilation or disappearance. With no background in existence, the "object" is born. We can now deal with "things" without considering the context in which they appear. We also can go a step further and use the objects as background and have common characteristics standing out as foreground and isolate them by annihilating, or bracketing off, the background. Such a process is called abstracting. Objects and abstractions are artifacts which give us some permanent usable events in contrast to the hazardous appearance of figure/background events. They are further fixed by specific sounds (words), which are then used (as symbols) to create new constellations (anecdotes, stories, poems, theses).

In the two processes of eating and of abstracting, we appropriate the world. In eating, however, we take something out of the world, which then actually disappears from the field. In abstracting and objectivizing (these being activities of the fantasy), we leave the field intact. Abstracting is not subtracting. (During these processes the background receives a negative, the foreground a positive cathexis. In these processes we say "yes" to the foreground and "no" to the background. The Cybernetics people have acknowledged the yes/no principle as the basic selective function of the organism and have succeeded in building very complicated and efficient machines on this principle.)

And indeed (though this is not visible at the first glance) we have two kinds of cathexis of the field: the positive attraction of

From Planned Psychotherapy to Gestalt Therapy

"impatience" and the negative repulsion of the "dread." We also have a great number of combinations of the two.

The "dreadful" is experienced as vague, undifferentiated danger. As soon as there is an object to cope with, dread diminishes into fear. As the positive cathexis indicates the life-supporting supplements, so negative cathexis indicates danger, indicates diminished support, or even death. In any case, it threatens that some or all of our existence is at stake, be it the physical being (illness), sexual integrity (castration), self-concept (humiliation), *weltaunschauung* (existential confusion), security (economic depression), and so forth.

The positive objects have to be appropriated, owned, and assimilated for homeostasis and support. (But, of course, homeostasis itself is a most powerful support for further development.) In contrast to this, we have to annihilate whatever has a negative cathexis; we have to remove it from the field. This applies to the actual field as it is involved in our fantasy. Bad thoughts, unwanted emotions, have to be removed from the danger field "as if" they were actual enemies.

The safest way to annihilate the enemy is to destroy him or render him harmless. This means destroying those means that support his threat to us. The next best thing in our "moving against" (Karen Horney) would be to frighten or threaten him, to chose him out of the danger zone. But this requires permanent vigilance. The pious person is always an guard against the devil.

★   ★   ★   ★   ★

In addition to destruction, we can cope with the negatively cathected situation by magic annihilation or by flight from the danger field. Both are *means of withdrawal*.

From Planned Psychotherapy to Gestalt Therapy

Magic annihilation corresponds to the proverbial ostrich, and is well known in psychoanalysis under the name of *scotoma*, that is, "blind spot." Children who don't want to listen to the sermons of the grown-ups like to cover their ears with their hands; if they don't want to see what they don't want to see, they shut their eyes tightly and, lo, the unpleasant thing has disappeared. Later they learn to "make their minds a blank" or to "forget it." Once such an attitude becomes widespread and habitual, then they become largely desensitized; they lose their senses, often when they need them most, as in recognizing danger.

Magic annihilation is a partial withdrawal. It is a substitute for actual withdrawal.

Withdrawal is another of the misunderstood problems of modern psychiatry. In this respect, it resembles the condemnation of sex in Freud's time and the disapproval of aggression in our time. The re-evaluation of sex is very much in vogue. The issue of aggression has been dealt with extensively in a previous publication. A reorientation of the withdrawal phenomenon will be more readily acceptable.

Common to all three phenomena is the fact that they are normal healthy occurrences, but that they all lend themselves easily to pathological distortions. Thus, if we talk about a withdrawn person, we have to realize that withdrawal per se is not a sign of neurosis or psychosis. We have to ask: withdrawn from what; permanently or temporarily withdrawn; withdrawn to what?

The same applies to the opposite of withdrawal, namely contact. We must emphasize that not all forms of contact are good. No doubt you have known people in your experience who have to stay in continual contact with you, the hangers-on. Every psychiatrist knows that they can make and have as much trouble as the deeply withdrawn. We know that some people just have to stay in contact with their fixed ideas; they cannot let go. Here we also have to ask:

From Planned Psychotherapy to Gestalt Therapy

contact *with* what and *for* what? We have called the contact with irrelevant activity the "dummy complex."

Not every contact is good and not every withdrawal bad. On the contrary, it is essential for every neurosis that the person cannot organize his withdrawal. The best example for this, perhaps, is the phenomenon of boredom. Boredom occurs when you try to stay in contact with a subject that does not hold your interest. You quickly exhaust any excitement at your disposal and get tired and lean back; you want to withdraw from the situation. If you cannot find a suitable excuse, the over-contact becomes painful — you are bored to tears or to death. If you let the tiredness take over, you will withdraw to your fantasy, to a more interesting contact. That your tiredness is merely a matter of very temporary exhaustion will be apparent from the enlivened interest when you suddenly find yourself leaning forward toward a more fascinating speaker. You will find yourself once more "all there."

We cannot consider withdrawing out of context. We must view it as a part of the contact/withdrawal process. Similarly, magnetism exists only in a context of a positive/negative field. Indeed, in the organism/environment field the positive and negative cathexes behave very similarly to the attractive and repelling forces of magnetism. As a matter of fact, the whole field is one unit which is dialectically differentiated. It is differentiated biologically into the organism and the environment, psychologically into the Self and the Otherness, morally into selfishness and altruism, scientifically into subjective and objective.

It is no wonder, then, that we experience any cathexis either subjectively or objectively. *We* either desire something or this something *has* an attraction for us; we are disgusted with something, or it *is* repellent.

For those interested in Gestalt psychology, we might add that the notion of the figure standing out in relief against the more indif-

From Planned Psychotherapy to Gestalt Therapy

ferent background needs some amplification from the same point of view. The outstanding figure is already a result of the pull between organism and positive cathexis. In negative cathexis the background becomes the foreground and the figure becomes background; it is pushed back; we want to remove the disturber from the scene. We feel like pushing someone's face, throwing him out of the window; we wish he would go away, for instance, to hell.

Linguistically, the positive cathexis is often indicated by the derivatives of the Latin *ad*, e.g., *acceptance, affection, affinity, appetite*; the negative cathexis by *re*, such as *rejection, regression, repulsion*. Of these, "acceptance" and "rejection" have become part of everyday psychiatric jargon. They certainly belong to psychopathology, once they appear as projections — such as the need to be accepted and the fear of being rejected. They will be discussed later in the context of "external support."

To accept and to reject are the dialectical components of discrimination and, as such, the most important functions of the self, that is, of contact/withdrawal functions, the rhythm of life. During the day we are in touch with the world; at night we withdraw. In summer we are more outgoing than in winter, when some animals take to a nearly complete withdrawal, to hibernation.

Of great importance is the amplitude of the contact/withdrawal rhythm. If the contact is over-prolonged, for example, in looking, vision becomes staring and, as such, ineffectual. One does not look any more, one looks through, one actually withdraws into a hypnotic trance. Similarly, in fighting: after he has contacted the jaw of his opponent, the boxer does not leave his fist there; he withdraws for the next blow, but he withdraws only out of reach. In sexual intercourse, too much contact is hurting; too much withdrawal is "interruption of the ongoing process." The stronger the orgasm, the greater is the amplitude of the jerking of

From Planned Psychotherapy to Gestalt Therapy

the pelvis, with deep exhalation and sound production alternating with relaxation and deep inhalation.

We are still left with a number of questions. Contact with what and for what? Withdrawal to where? To answer these questions, we have to return to the discussion of the instinct circuit and we have to take up the notion of support. But first, one more word about emotions.

Just as we debunked the notion of "mind," so science has done with the totality of our feelings which was called the soul and given the status of immortality; Any revolution, including the scientific one, behaves cybernetically, that is, it first swings too much to the dialectic opposite. This happened, for instance, with ideas about sex. Where previously all neurotic evil was attributed to sex, now it is often relegated to the *repression* of it. So with the soul. Its divinity has been turned into a nuisance. A mother who grieves loudly about a lost child "has an emotional breakdown." Emotions nowadays have to be discharged as if they were a bothersome surplus.

Indeed, nature is not so wasteful as to create emotions for such a purpose. The ideal might be to make well-adjusted robots from feeling humans, and parents and psychiatrists might think wishfully that one could get rid of emotions by discharge. But look at the results: empty personalities who are a bore to themselves and everybody around them.

No, emotions are the very life of us. Many theories have been brought forward to explain and interpret emotions. But emotions do not have to be explained, much less interpreted. They are the very language of the organism; they modify the basic excitement according to the situation which has to be met. If you want a label for my fantasy about the total process, you might call it "The Transformation Theory." Excitement is transformed into specific emotions, and emotions are transformed into sensoric and motoric action. The emotions energize the cathexis and mobilize the ways and means to complete the instinct circuits. It is amazing, when the process is carried through, how the felt emotions disappear and how the blind emotions turn into a clear appraisal of the opportunities of the field.

*   *   *   *   *

In the organism's pursuit of the cathected object, we come across another of the ever-intruding philosophical questions, another of the either/or situations. Do we live by free will or by causal determination?

Freud's investigations were motivated by his lack of will-power, by the weakness and passivity of his Ego. And indeed, if we look at our New Year's resolutions or the determination of the alcoholic to stop drinking, we can take only a dim view of man's capacity to control himself.

On the other hand, the law demands full responsibility for our actions lest we be declared of unsound mind. And we ourselves demand it. Otherwise we would not be so full of excuses and rationalizations. We seem truly to be caught between necessity and freedom.

I believe a look at the manipulation of the instinct circuits will provide an answer to this dilemma. The goal is fixed; it represents the necessity. The supplement needed by the organism to restore its balance does not leave us much freedom. However, we have a certain freedom in the means of achieving this goal. Not the freedom of the will, although there is the deliberate "interruption of the on-going process," but a freedom of choice, an opening up of possibilities. In other words, our freedom does not stem from the system of manipulation, but from better orientation, from a perspective, or seeing possibilities.

From Planned Psychotherapy to Gestalt Therapy

The necessity may be to send a message to a relative. The possibilities are to send it by wire, by telephone, by letter, or through another person. Which possibility one selects depends on decision, natural preference, or habit.

Right now I feel such a choice. I feel very much tempted to talk about decision, confusion and despair, all of which have to do with a bad technique of selecting. I also feel the wish to discuss semantics and to point out that meanings are "means" and not goals. Thus, in order to get the just-mentioned message across, one has to select the means — technical as well as symbolic — that is, one has to choose the right words.

How can we speak of the instincts working as necessities if we are not even aware of them? We have spoken of the futility of trying to classify instincts. But is our assumption of a great number of instincts not just a mere personal fantasy? How do we know that instincts exist at all?

We don't know, but we take the striving toward or against and away from the cathected object as an absolute necessity, and we do the same with the symptoms, the signs of the assumed instincts. We do not feel the dehydration, but we feel a dry mouth and we feel the pull toward some fluid. That is all we are aware of. Peculiarly, though the needed supplement has a positive cathexis, the symptoms are of a negative character; the dry mouth or whatever indicates the need is felt as painful and has to be annihilated, so much so that we frequently go astray in our endeavors and deal with the annihilation of symptoms without achieving the required homeostasis, without finishing the situation as required. Unfinished business which has insomnia for a symptom is not completed by taking sleeping pills.

Consequently, the whole theory of Freud about repression of instincts collapses. We can never, never repress any instinct whatsoever, because it is out of reach of our awareness and thus out of

From Planned Psychotherapy to Gestalt Therapy

reach of any deliberate action. However, we can, and do very frequently, interfere with the signs and symptoms, with the consummation of those unwanted strivings. This is done by "interrupting the on-going process." Such interruptions can be effected at any stage of the (often very intricate) execution of the instinct circuit. We can and do interrupt the contact as well as the withdrawal needs. It is important to note that the neurotic suffers not only from inadequate contact, but likewise from incomplete withdrawal; for instance, he remains tense, where he could relax his vigilance; he suffers from insomnia, when he requires rest.

Self-interruptions can readily be observed. The "er . . . er" and "uh" of any self-conscious speaker, the incomplete sentences, the gaps within sentences, may irritate you as much as an interrupted gesture. Your neighbor at the dinner table stretches out his hand for the sugar and stops it in mid-air, asking you whether you take sugar with your coffee. He looks at you and immediately interrupts the visual contact by withdrawing his eyes, for he begins to feel embarrassed. A very important interruption is interfering with the transformation of basic excitement into specific emotions. Again the interference is executed against the aware symptoms, since all the self-preaching ("now, don't get excited !") helps not one whit. Instead, one stops breathing, holds the diaphragm, diverts one's attention. And then one of the fundamental neurotic symptoms, anxiety, comes into being. Thus, anxiety is not repressed libido, or repressed aggression, or repressed death instinct, or repressed exhibitionism; or repressed expressionism; it is any one of these or other possibilities. It is, practically speaking, the inability to take the step to any emotional involvement. One is anxious to be oneself, but afraid to, for the self is the ever-flowing, ever-changing emotional engagement and disengagement with and from the world about us. Love, hate and peace; impatience, dread and interest; appetite, frustration and satisfaction; expectation, disappointment

From Planned Psychotherapy to Gestalt Therapy

and appreciation; guilt, resentment and gratitude, are some of the triangles of our life; they are the dialectical opposites and their integration.

Freud's attitude toward self-interruption is most relevant. Of all possible interruptions, he chose a very decisive one, and called it the Censor. He said: "Do not interrupt the free flow of your associations!" But he also assumed that the censor was the servant of embarrassment, and thus spoke Freud. "Do not be embarrassed!" Precisely with these two taboos he interrupted the experience and dissolving of embarrassment, resulting in a desensitization of it, or even (and this applies even more to the Reichian patients) in over-compensating brazenness. What has to be tackled in therapy is not the censored material but, in this instance, the specific form of interrupting, namely, the censoring itself.

Self-interruption is not a human invention for the sake of self-control. What is human is the retroflection, turning toward oneself the dreaded element. Interruption is thus another way, besides destroying and withdrawing, to cope with a true or imagined danger. To get the full significance of interrupting, one may look at the examples of warfare. Bombers are sent out to interrupt the flow of supplies by destroying railways and trucks; artillery and rifles are used to stop the enemy from personal (for instance, bayonet) contact. The enemy, on the other hand, will not only do the same; he will also interrupt the interrupter.

You have experienced telephone interruptions. You have experienced what a nuisance people can be when they interrupt your work (but only if you are really interested; otherwise, the interrupter is welcome) or your dreaming or your sleep. You have come to dread such people and are impatient to get rid of them.

Do interruptions always leave us with the need to finish situations? According to the homeostatic principle, yes. And yet we know that there is another possibility open in many cases-a withdrawal from the unfinished situation, for instance, in the form of resignation. There is a false resignation, a giving-in with a sigh, but this is a form of self-interruption, leaving the situation still open to be resumed at a later date. True resignation can be accomplished with pseudo-instincts by withdrawing, and it can be accomplished with true needs, with a part of the self, by genuine grief, by accomplishing a thorough assimilation, by what Freud calls the mourning labor. Grief is necessary, internal destruction, de-structuring a part of the self, for instance, that part that was in close relationship with a deceased friend.

Take the case of a man who has lost a leg and bears it with a smile and a stiff upper lip. Any depression or unhappiness he begins to develop is cut short with a grim determination to "adjust" himself. He still considers himself a two-legged man with one missing leg and will find himself again and again in positions where he feels this loss and bears it. If he goes through the mourning labor, however, his present self will die. It is not sufficient to bear the cross; he has to go through the crucifixion in order to be resurrected as a new and different organism, as a one-legged organism with a difference balance and potential than he had before. Now his energies are no longer tied up in his heroic struggle; now he is free to grow again and to transcend his handicap; as for the new self, this is not much more of a handicap than that we feel in the absence of six octopus legs.

Another man had lost his father and had not shed more than a trickle of tears over him. He said he felt relieved that the old man who had regulated his life was dead. But just the opposite is true. By not mourning he keeps him alive; he has "introjected" the old man; he fantasizes him still around within himself, fantasizes him still giving orders, and he still needs him for support on decisions. He is no more free of him than before his death. Only after working through his loss, his aloneness, perhaps his loneliness, can he be

From Planned Psychotherapy to Gestalt Therapy

115

reborn as what he is, not a rebellious orphan, but a lost soul without opinions of his own, an adult man, but in need of the "external
support" of guidance.

Both persons had chronically interrupted the on-going process
of the self. Both had interfered with their development.

Note the *inter* in *inter*rupt and *inter*fere, also in *inter*vene and
*inter*cept, the putting of something between. It is obvious now that
the therapeutic procedure (which is the re-establishment of the self
by integrating the dissociated parts of the personality) must be the
teaching of "non-interruption." How can we do this without making the mistake of interrupting the interruption? We have previously mentioned Freud's command: "Do not censor," which is
itself a censoring of the censor, an interruption of the process of
censoring.

In a neurosis we (in psychoanalytical language the Ego) interrupt our selves (usually spelled ourselves). To interrupt the enemy
is, as we have seen, an essential survival activity. When we interrupt ourselves, we may also succeed in disrupting our selves, even
if we are not "our own worst enemies."

Just as in the Freudian case, where we censor ourselves rather
than the "other," so with interrupting. A boy gets a moral sermon
from his headmaster; he wants to interrupt him. Or a beating: he
would like still more to interrupt that. Instead, in both instances he
interrupts the expressions of the self (and there is nothing unconscious about this), which in the first case would be a sentence like:
"I resent your bawling me out," or in the second instance, a wish to
kick. He has to interrupt, but he interrupts his own expressions; he
"controls himself," since he cannot control the headmaster. He has
to stifle his impatience (anger), for he is in dread of the consequences of self-expression.

From Planned Psychotherapy to Gestalt Therapy

We interrupt, of course, not only the "moving against" but likewise the "towards" and "away" tendencies. We interrupt not only the contacting but likewise the withdrawing.

For example, your host has buttonholed you and bombards you with a lot of "Why's" and "Doctor-how-do-you-explain-that's?" You feel very much like withdrawing from him, but your politeness or, if you are neurotic, your fear of hurting his feelings intervenes. If, in addition, your withdrawal is meant to find a more fascinating contact in the next room, your self-interference will turn into resentment. But resentment is, as will be shown later, a no-man's-land emotion. As the situation is, you cannot make contact with your host, which would mean playing the wise guy who knows all the answers, nor can you withdraw from him, nor can you make the contact that appears to be relevant at this moment to you. You are stuck in a no-man's-land; you are "neither here nor there."

What is the advantage of changing over from considering the censor to dealing with interruptions? First of all, psychoanalysis is not very much concerned with the censor, that is, with the aware part of the on-going process, but rather with the material which is being censored. Even though Freud points to the importance of embarrassment, little is said about the phenomenology, experience and treatment of embarrassment and many other emotions, though one has to record some notable exceptions, such as grief and affection. If one deals with interruptions, however, one deals with the clinical picture right in front. There is no need to guess and to interpret. We hear the interruption of a sentence; we notice that the patient holds his breath. We see that he is making a fist or swinging his legs "as if" he felt a desire to kick and did not complete it; we observe how he interrupts the visual contact and looks away from us. When the psychoanalyst interprets the unconscious for the patient, he aims at increasing the patient's awareness, but he

From Planned Psychotherapy to Gestalt Therapy

diminishes the patient's tendencies to increase that awareness and the initiative to do so. On the contrary, by doing the run toward the train or the bus, but we block that by our reason, or by the dread that we might miss it altogether. At the same time we cannot withdraw from this impatience (for our omnipotence is at stake), keep the fact of waiting in the background and, in the meantime, find some interest in the posters or a book or in the other people waiting. Of course, the less impatience, the easier for another interest to occupy the foreground. We become aware of our impatience on account of the frustrating situation; we become aware of it because the transformation of impatience into activity is interrupted.

The impatience about the train definitively shows all the signs of a dominance over any other activity, and we behave thus I "as if" this was the most important survival instinct at that moment. This again seems to be inconsistent with our biological concept of homeostasis and instinct circuit. Yet once the train has arrived, the tension is transformed into gladness and relief, just as with any instinctual satisfaction. It would be rather absurd to assume that we are born with a "subway instinct." It would likewise be no less absurd to regress to Freudian symbolism and assume a libidinal excitement for witnessing the phallic train rushing through the maternal vagina. Many analysts, bound by the necessity of their training and squeezed into the Procrustes-bed of their theories, have opportunistically taken such a view.

At least two instances are known to us where objects receive a cathexis equivalent to instinctual cathexis. The first are events which during our lifetime have acquired an existential significance, events which have produced imperatives which are on a par with biological instincts. These are, however, not grounded in physiology but in fantasy; they are articles of faith. We could call them pseudo-instincts, because they behave as if they were absolutes, necessities. Under favorable circumstances notwithstanding, they

From Planned Psychotherapy to Gestalt Therapy

might turn into choices. One might discover that me can do without satisfying them and the roof still does not cave in. Perhaps the best example of this is the taboo of the primitive. The vagueness of the dreadful is fastened onto some possibility, and these are as numerous as tribes in existence. But once such a possibility is chosen as the seat of the dreadful, there is hardly any choice except to obey or to perish. In other words, the taboo assumes the importance of the only means to avert an "existential crisis," a significance similar to any of the survival instincts of the living organism.

Rituals, for instance those of the obsessional character, have a similar but somewhat faded intensity. Obsessions, sexual fetishism, fixed ideas, superstitions, self-concepts, moral principles, and many more rigid forms of behavior fall into the same category of pseudo-instincts.

Especially significant for our purpose is the fact that every neurosis is, like the taboo, a device designed to avert an existential crisis. Therapy is the facilitation of the development of the patient, who has to learn to cope with the exigencies of life in such a way that the fantasy of the "existential crisis" collapses.

Before we discuss the notion of the existential crisis, we have to take up the second instance of situations which receive a cathexis equivalent to instincts. These situations are, in the language of John Dewey and F. M. Alexander, the "means whereby" for the "end gain"; they are, in our language, the support functions for adequate contact and withdrawal.

In the movies recently I saw a beaver defending himself against a wolf. The wolf, afraid of the very sharp teeth, ran around the little fellow with great agility. The beaver's means of orientation were good enough; he perceived well every movement of the enemy, but he could not turn around quickly enough to use his only means of protection, his teeth. He was too clumsy; his coordination, though sufficient in water, was inadequate for this fight on

From Planned Psychotherapy to Gestalt Therapy

land. His turning-around speed was not good support for defense, just as the speed of his legs, previously, was insufficient for flight, for withdrawal into the water. It was no match for the wolf's.

Here is an excellent illustration that it is not only ungratified instincts that lead to an existential crisis, with the possibility of what Goldstein calls a catastrophical reaction. We have here the frequent case of the "means whereby" or the support of the instinct cycle having the same significance as the instincts themselves, because insufficient support is as much a threat to life as are ungratified instincts. A chain is as weak as its weakest link. In the completion of the instinct circuit, every step in orientation as well as in manipulation must be readily at our disposal. For good living, good coordination, timing, grace and ease of performance are needed. We have to develop good habits of perceiving and acting.

The human organism is a highly complicated organization. The advantage of the human compared with other animals is that he has tools and symbols at his disposal. This certainly helps him in his fight against other animals, and it helps him to plunder Mother Earth. It prevents many existential crises by giving him safety, protection from epidemics, etc., and it gives him security such as insurance policies.

But on the other side of the ledger, we have two facts: the individual safety is bought at a price of collective insecurity, and the individual ability to handle emergency situations degenerates swiftly, so much so that people are becoming more and more helpless and less and less self- supportive. In short, they become neurotic, for neurosis is the illness of lacking self-support.

★   ★   ★   ★   ★

Growth and development are characterized by at least two phenomena, by the transformation of novelty into routine, as in

From Planned Psychotherapy to Gestalt Therapy

habit formation or acquiring skill, and by the replacement of environmental support by self-support. These two tendencies overlap to a considerable extent, for instance, in discovering where after a time we can dispense with the external support of the teacher and select and devise our own course of study.

The replacement of external by internal support applies to all animals. The more differentiated they are, the longer they rely on external, mostly maternal support. The gradual replacement of external by self-support is the essence of maturation, that is, to be one's age. Thus, another of today's psychiatric dichotomies has to be rejected: the maturity/infantilism split. A child of seven might want to be spoon-fed or carried when he should be able to feed himself and to walk. But he does not behave according to his age. The maturity/infantilism split concept is largely due to the Freudian idea of infantile regression, which in plainer English means withdrawal to a state of childhood. Freud also realized that this regression was incomplete, and he designed his treatment accordingly. He wanted to reach the point in the child's development where the hitch occurred that had stopped further growth.

Our objection here is merely the confusion of genus with species, of some" and "all." "Some" neuroses show this withdrawal to infancy but not "all"; on the other hand, "all" organisms withdraw and not just "some" neurotics. As can readily be observed, some withdrawals occur behind very elaborate and mature defenses. Infantile regression can also be a very deliberate action. Playing the baby is a trick often used by platinum blond "babes" to get fur coats from "sugar daddies." There is nothing unconscious about putting on such an act.

The same can be said about infantile trauma. A trauma is an injury, and an injury heals, if there is no permanent disorganization to keep it alive. "Some" traumata produce such a state, mostly via creating states of confusion, but not "all." "Some" permanent

From Planned Psychotherapy to Gestalt Therapy

disorganizations are created not by traumata but, for instance, by inconsistent behavior of parents by making demands the child cannot cope with. These, too, are likely to create areas of confusion, which are about as important with neurotics as they are with psychotics. They are only better dissimulated. To become aware of and to dissolve such areas of confusion is an important part of psychotherapy.

Areas of confusion are bad support for good contact. They show symptoms such as embarrassment, panic, de-"cisions," even despair. The patient very often is unaware of such states of confusion, but the therapist apparently has two signs at his disposal to reach these areas: the blotting out and the psychosomatic manifestations. We shall have opportunity to discuss them in greater detail in connection with therapy.

We have, of course, the need to encapsulate such disturbing events as confusion. They, like many other events (mainly retroflections, introjections and projections), interfere with good support. They considerably diminish the organism's potential. We cannot apply ourselves to the best of our abilities, nor can we enjoy life as we could without the neurotic ballast. This ballast, however, is a nuisance only as long as it is dissociated from the self. Once integrated, it contributes to the self-support to a truly unbelievable degree.

Imagine a kitten climbing a tree, enjoying the experimenting with balancing and testing, but the mother cat insisting that it will break its neck. How much this would interfere with its pleasure in hunting! But cats, of course, are not that stupid. They leave the pursuit of safety and the deadening of the self-preserving instincts to the humans. On the contrary, the cat, like any other animal and any sensible human being, will consider as the essence of up- bringing the facilitation of transforming external into self-support. It is not mainly affection that the infant needs. Too much affection will spoil and suffocate the child, especially when the parent is loaded with too much libido and possessiveness. Then, instead of encouraging self-support, the parents will condition the child to rely too much on their help.

The newly born kitten can neither feed, transport nor defend itself. For all this it needs its mother. But it will develop the means to do these things itself, partly through developing its inborn instincts, and partly through environmental teaching. In the human being, the transition from external to self-support is, of course, more complicated. Consider only the need to change diapers, to dress, to cook, to earn money, to choose a vocation, to gain knowledge.

Since we are forced to learn so much more through education than by using our inherited instincts, much of the intuition as to what is the right procedure is missing. Instead, the "right" procedure is established by composite fantasies which are handed over and modified from generation to generation. They are mostly support functions for social contact, such as manners and codes of behavior (ethics), means to orientation (reading, *weltanschauungen*), standards of beauty (esthetics), social position (avocation). Often, however, they are not biologically orientated (they are even sometimes anti-biological), thus disrupting the very roots of our existence and leading to degeneration and, finally, to the downfall of those nations who overdo the anti-biological education. The different languages express their attitudes toward such interfering processes. In English what is not "right" has to be "left" abandoned. The French *gauche* stresses the awkwardness of such halving and malcoordination. The German *linkisch* means the same, actually disjointed. The Romans underlined the scotoma nature and called the left *sinister,* the dark.

In therapy, we shall have to reintegrate the social and the biological functions, if they are contradictory. We have to establish

From Planned Psychotherapy to Gestalt Therapy

ambidexterity, so that right and left support each other. Even with the left-handed, a great deal can be done by finding and removing the interruptions of the right. Much more frequently we find suppression of left-hand activities. Let the left hand know very much what the right hand is doing. There is no need to fight life "single-handed."

Just as we need coordination of right and left, we need (probably much more) the coordination of the upper and lower parts of ourselves.

Dr. Laura Perls, who first worked out the relationship of contact and support, found an especially interesting case in human posture. Here something exists that at first glance looks like another dichotomy, an apparent division of contact (for the upper) and support (for the lower part). Let us, for the time being, follow this pseudo-split, but emphasize that always there is a development from contact to support, for the "end gain" to become "means" for new "end gains." And let us further state that from now on, we shall refer to the contact-withdrawal rhythm merely as contact. Withdrawal is the disengagement from contact and requires good support as such. For an orderly withdrawal, an army requires as much food, roads, coordination and morale as for advance. Without such support, there looms the threat of an "existential crisis," the danger of disintegration. The army may cease to be an army and become a mere flock of soldiers. The classical example is Napoleon's retreat from Moscow, when the Russians won merely by depriving his army of its life-supporting requirements. Only those soldiers survived who managed to support themselves.

I believe that the evolutionary leap of homo sapiens was due to his change of posture, though preceded in the ape by an important differentiation of the hands. While most animals use their limbs for walking and standing, the ape can walk on his hind limbs, and he can climb and hang on the tree with one or more limbs. At the same time, the hands differentiate into a four-and-a-thumb finger division, thereby making the hands into very useful tools. In the human being, the differentiation goes further. The hands can now take over many "mani"pulations which were previously done awkwardly by the mouth. This is probably due to a better use of the senses, as with the erect position the senses are geared for better perspective. They are freer, removed from the closeness of the ground. Due to removing his head from close to the ground, man sees more, but he smells less.

Man's erect position makes for greater alertness and agility. To appreciate the importance of this, could you imagine walking for just one day on all fours? How little would we accomplish with our hands; and we would have to re-install the mouth for many actions. It is also a provocative experiment not to use the thumb for a while; one soon realizes that it is as important as the other four fingers together.

Instead of the solid support of four limbs, we are relying on a more precarious balance. Now balance is a very subtle action requiring a great deal of fine coordination. Any chronic muscular contraction, such as occurs in what Reich calls the "motoric armor" endangers this coordination, especially when the center of gravity, the pelvis, is unfree, mostly due to anal and genital contractions and desensitizations.

If ease of balance is missing, if there is insufficient self-support, we look for external support. In extreme cases we need braces and crutches; otherwise, frequent leaning against the wall or the furniture or sitting down relieves the strain which bad postural habits induce. Healthy striving is always in the direction of self-support. The baby relies first on his mother's hands or holds onto the playpen. The man who needs a crutch after a leg injury will discard it as soon as possible, unless he needs it for neurotic reasons (to secure

From Planned Psychotherapy to Gestalt Therapy

external support, for instance, attention, pity, service, or health insurance payments).

Not every instance of external support is pathological. The middle aged person needing glasses because he has become too far-sighted, the truly sick person, the man who realizes that a job can-not be done single- handed-they should not all try to be self-sup-portive.

In these and other cases we would have to use another word: self-sufficient. To be self-sufficient is often a matter of spite, how-ever: "I can do it all by myself." Masturbation, for example, is a demonstration of self-sufficiency, but it can also be a symptom of lacking libidinal support for adequate contact. It is not always easy to distinguish whether we deal with a symptom of self-sufficiency, that is, of withdrawal, or of self-support, that is, of contact.

The essence of good contact/support relationship lies in its promotion of growth and development. What is contact today will be assimilated via routine or habit formation and will serve as good support for tomorrow's contact. This applies to all aspects of or-ganic life, to the physiological functions as well as to emotions, intellect, skill, habits, etc. To make good visual contact, that is, to see well, we must have the support of good structure and function of our optical system. To have good inter-personal relations, we need the support of interest in other people and of self-expression. For otherwise, how can we reach each other? The therapist who considers clients as "cases" will not be successful, as he is not in contact with his patients but only with his academic gown of dig-nity and superiority.

Often when he, or any person who is wearing a front, wants to be himself, he has to interrupt whatever he is doing or feeling. Such masks or pretenses very often amount to the formation of an anti-self, which likewise requires the permanent support of the person. Such anti-self formations, for instance, an ego-ideal or a self-concept, are mostly reaction formations to the true self; but as their support does not come from deep biological layers, they are anti-survival and interfere with good contact. One is withdrawn behind one's mask, and only the mask is in contact with the world.

From Planned Psychotherapy to Gestalt Therapy

Morality, Ego Boundary, and Aggression

Reprinted from Complex, #9, 1955, pp. 42-52

The idea of absolute morality, the conviction that good and bad do exist and that what is good or bad is fixed once and for all, is as old as human culture. In the Bible the snake tempts Adam with the promise that he can, by eating an apple, know good and bad. (Note that he acquires such knowledge by eating.) Even such a man of the Enlightenment as Sigmund Freud shows traces of such an idea when he says, "The Unconscious is not always bad; sometimes it is better than the conscious person." Psychoanalytical investigations show indeed that at least our consciences behave as if there were an absolute morality; conscience evaluates our deeds as good and bad. The absoluteness of morality has a tremendous advantage. It provides the believer with a sense of security. He knows how to act, he knows what is right and wrong. The law demands from a sane person that he should be able to distinguish right and wrong. He may not like it, but he can avoid doubt and stay out of "trouble."

The idea of the relativity of morality is not new either. The proofs of it are so overwhelming that we can hardly understand why mankind has been going along suffering the notions of sin and guilt, often driven to despair, suicide, saintliness, insanity, or voluntary incarceration. But we truly suspend between the two poles: the uncertainty of relative morals and the despair of absolute morality, between the Scylla of reason and the Charybdis of revelation.

Is there a way out for us? Can we find a unifying absoluteness behind the relativity of morality, a point of view from which faith, conviction and rationality can be unified? I believe so; but I do not think it can be done without attaining a new attitude toward aggression. Morality and aggression, I intend to show, are essentially linked. We may consider absolute and relative morality with respect to the total personality or the situation. In the story of *Dr. Jekyll and Mr. Hyde*, the total personality is good or bad. It is even represented by two people with two names. So in ordinary language we say, "He is a different person," "You are a bad boy," "She used to be such a nice person," "You are a liar." In each case we identify the total personality. Consider the devastating consequences of this kind of as-if-identification: label your child a liar a few times for having a vivid fantasy life, and he will feel under the obligation to live up to the epithet "liar"; he will actually become a chronic liar, if mother says so, because mother knows best. As to situations, think of the Victorian morality and compare then and now. The best theme for comparison is the attitude toward sex. The condemnation of sex at that time was so strong that "immoral" meant sexually immoral. Compare the Victorian ideal with our ideal. The Victorian ideal was to be beautiful, chaste, and thrifty; the present American ideal is to be glamorous, sexy, and efficient. Because of economic independence and the ever-deepening conflict

From Planned Psychotherapy to Gestalt Therapy

between religion and science, the simplicity of faith and the greediness of progress, the social situation has altered.

From the psychiatrist's point of view, we can say that on the whole the battle against neurosis-producing sex-repression has been won, but a great many mopping-up operations still remain to be done. For instance, while the quantity of sex is abundant, the quality of the sexual act as the most intimate and intense expression of love leaves much to be desired. Instead of satisfaction and gratitude we find emptiness and disgust, frigidity and perversions as the companions of what is meant to be the ecstatic climax of human experience. The danger of today's outlook is this: while in Victorian times most of the evil was attributed to sex, we now attribute it too easily to the repression of sex.

Yet we may safely say that in the sexual sphere there is less misery. We can now press on to the next bogeyman of mankind, aggression, which is now regarded as being the "root of all evil." Aggression shares this place with money, but I am of the opinion that the curse of money cannot be solved until we come to a better understanding of aggression. For instance, let me merely mention that without solving the riddle of aggression we cannot understand greed.

There is an interesting mixture of relative and absolute morality within the individual. We use the expression "double standard"; this means that we have two yardsticks of moral measurement, one for ourselves and one for the others. "Quod licet Jovi, non beet Bovi" — what is permissible for Jupiter is forbidden to cows. In psychiatry we find an illness that has this double morality as its main symptom. I mean paranoia. The paranoiac is always a moralist, and very proud of it. He is unfairly treated, victimized, wronged, but he does not realize for a moment that he is doing all the victimizing and wronging. But we all have such double standards, though some of us are adept at covering up with good rationalizations.

From Planned Psychotherapy to Gestalt Therapy

For a physician and a psychologist the problem of morality boils down to one question: can we, dissatisfied with absolute and relative morality, find an unequivocal answer in the morality of the organism? Can we find, on the nonverbal level, experiences that can be labeled good and bad? If there are such experiences and they occur as a normal process, we can make them the basis of a useful morality — I might even go so far as to say that an objective outlook without evaluation is an impossibility.

My contention is that there *is* such a morality of the organism. Good and bad are responses of the organism. But the *label* "good" or "bad" is then unfortunately projected onto the stimulus; then, isolated, torn out of context, these labels are organized into codes of conduct, systems of morals, often legalized, and connected with religious cosmologies. Let us take this up piecemeal.

Good and bad are responses of the organism. We say, "You make me mad," "You make me feel happy," less frequently, "You make me feel good," "You make me feel bad." Among primitive people such phrases occur with extreme frequency. Again we use expressions like "I feel good" "I feel lousy," without considering the stimulus. But what is happening is that an ardent pupil makes his teacher feel good, an obedient child makes his parents feel good. The victorious boxer makes his fan feel good, as does the efficient lover his mistress. A book or a picture does the same when it meets your aesthetic needs. And *vice versa:* if people or objects fail to meet needs and produce satisfaction, we feel bad about them.

The next step is that instead of owning up to our experiences as ours we project them and throw the responsibility for our own responses onto the stimulus. (This might be because we are afraid of our excitement, feel that we are failing in excitement, want to shirk responsibility, etc., etc.) We say the pupil, the child, the boxer, the lover, the book, the picture "is" good or bad. At that moment, labeling the stimulus good or bad, we cut off good and bad from our own experience. They become abstractions, and the stimulus-objects are correspondingly pigeonholed. This does not happen without consequences. Once we isolate thinking from feeling, judgment from intuition, morality from self-awareness, deliberateness from spontaneity, the verbal from the nonverbal, we lose the self, the essence of existence, and we become either frigid human robots or confused neurotics.

Nature has not provided us with the deep sense of feeling good or bad without deep meaning for survival; this emotional compass indicates a direction for us on even the most abstract and refined levels of existence. To speak in summary fashion: Feeling good for the organism means identification, be one with me; feeling bad means alienation, you go away. In the feeling of good and bad we see the discriminating function of the organism; this is a work of what we call, in Gestalt therapy, the ego boundary.

Let us consider the nature of this ego boundary. I want to make two points. (1) The ego boundary is flexible. In the healthy person it is changeable as situations change; but in psycho-pathological states it is rather rigid. Such rigidity looks as if it would make for stability, but the stability is the stability of a "principled" person who disregards his emotions and the evidence for the sake of his preconceived ideas. One of the greatest dangers of absolute morality is that it makes for rigid ego boundaries. (2) The ego boundary can be thought of as a meeting of opposite sets of emotions, acceptances and rejections, identifications and alienations, positive and negative emotions. Let us bear in mind that "I" is not a real existing object or a part of the organism. "I" is a symbol of a symbol. "I" indicates a state or a functioning. What underlies is more closely given in words like "intuition" or "mood." Like the indescribable something which we call the "mood" of a person, the "I" is experienceable but has no fixity.

From Planned Psychotherapy to Gestalt Therapy

When I say "I am here," I mean to say "Here is an organism in front of you with whose functions the speaker identifies himself." If this organism should say, for instance, "I didn't do it," there is an alienation, a "not I" involved.

Perhaps the basic function of the ego boundary is discrimination. And we can say that neurotic conflict is simply the conflict between two types of discrimination, an "introjected" or alien discrimination (somebody else's choosing that we have incorporated) and the discrimination of the organism. Karen Horney, for instance, spoke of the idealized image and Sullivan of the self-system as the introjected discrimination. Bergler, like many psychoanalysts before him, found the mainspring of conflict in conscience. Freud used the name superego.

Now peculiarly it has been overlooked that the conflict between these discriminations must involve aggression, for aggression is the essence of conflict. Without aggression, peace of mind would prevail. Thus, whatever the neurotic conflict may be about, we must first of all get hold of the aggression that causes and maintains the conflict.

Let us return to *Dr. Jekyll and Mr. Hyde*. In that story the conflict is apparently finished *as far as* the Doctor is concerned. He has disavowed all unwanted properties and has become an ideal. His discrimination has kept everything that was in his time considered to be good, and has projected everything bad onto Mr. Hyde. For instance, we can say that he has disowned his animal nature. His ego boundary runs between the two personalities. Everything inside the boundary is good, everything outside bad. We should actually call our hero Mr. X, for as you see by now, the Doctor and Mr. are two parts of a split person, and the split, the insulating layer, is the ego boundary. The idealist in this person, of course, would like to become a killer himself, namely to kill the animal nature in him, but this would mean suicide and the end of the story, for you cannot kill nature. More generally, on the inside of each ego boundary we find the cohesive forces of integration which we call good, and on the other side the destructive forces of aggression that we call bad. On the inside is what we accept and what is familiar, outside is what we reject as strange. The laws of the ego boundary, identification and alienation, apply to all boundary phenomena. They apply to interpersonal relations, as "you are mine," "I don't know you anymore," "This can't be my son." They apply intrapersonally as in Mr. X. We can fill whole books with examples of dissociations of parts of ourselves, due to repressions, projections, self-control, and other means of alienating the organismic discrimination. Identification and alienation occur in social organizations as well, a nation, a club, a racial group, a fraternity. The laws are especially pronounced where the "otherness" is stressed, as in nationalisms, cults, systems of exploitation or reform. The closer the inner ties of the members of a group, the more aggression and hostility gathers outside the boundaries. It is because the Montagues and Capulets are such cohesive clans that they are so hostile to each other. One's own god is always the good one. The strange god is rejected. One's own soldiers are brave heroes. The enemy is a raping villain.

Aggression and cohesion are mutually dependent. After the aggression of Pearl Harbor, the inner cohesion, the feeling of oneness within the United States, increased considerably, and the aggression hitherto invested in party and class strife went to the boundary as a powerful means of defense.

So we have quite naturally come to the theme of aggression. If one's discrimination calls whatever is outside the boundary bad, then a real danger arises. For the closer neighbors are in space or spirit, the greater is the danger of identification between them, which means a danger of losing one's own identity. So the need for destroying the threat arises. And, contrariwise, if a unit wants to expand, as in the growth of an individual personality or of a nation,

From Planned Psychotherapy to Gestalt Therapy

or the need of a reform movement to make proselytes, the unit needs aggression to destroy the resistance encountered. So let us discuss a moment this word "destroy."

We often think of destroying as annihilation, but we cannot destroy a substance important to us in such a way that it is made *nihil*, nothing. To destroy means to de-structure, to break into pieces. Aggression has a twofold purpose: first, to de-structure any threatening enemy to the point where he becomes impotent; and, second, in an expanding aggression, to de-structure the substance that is needed for growth and to render it assimilable. Even Hitler, when setting out to destroy Czechoslovakia, was careful not to destroy the armament factories that he wanted to incorporate into his greater Germany.

Thus aggression is essential for survival and growth. It is not an invention of the devil, but a means of nature. We can understand the wish of parents that aggression be merely a neurosis of naughty children, or of psychiatrists in mental hospitals that aggression can be discharged like a physical excretion, to get rid of something unpleasant. Actually nature is not so wasteful as to create such a powerful energy as aggression just to be "got rid of" or "abreacted." In cases of pathological aggression, we have simply instances of unorganized, useless aggression. As a tool of nature, aggression is valuable; as the tool of moralistic discrimination, it becomes an instrument for non-survival. For example, a case of nervous breakdown is due to too much self-control, and this means that the person is directing aggression against his own spontaneous impulses.

In order to live, an organism must grow, physically and mentally. To grow, we must incorporate external substance, and in order to make it assimilable, we have to de-structure it. Let us consider just the elementary tool of aggressive de-structuring, the teeth. To build up the highly differentiated proteins of human flesh,

From Planned Psychotherapy to Gestalt Therapy

we have to de-structure the molecules in our food. This occurs in three stages, biting, chewing, digesting. For biting, we have incisors, the front teeth, in our culture somewhat replaced by the cutting knife. The first step is the cutting of large pieces into morsels. Secondly, we grind down the morsels to a pulp with the help of our molars, or culturally, with millstones. (A patient told me he could not see anything aggressive in chewing, though he could in biting; but how would he feel if he were lying between two millstones?) Lastly, there is the chemical de-structuring in our stomachs, by means of dissolving acids. (For example, in cases of resentment, which is an incomplete aggression, we often have the effect of stomach ulcers.)

Not only the teeth, of course, are tools of aggression, but the muscles of the jaw, the hands, the words. The aggression is given in the organic working-together of all the parts of the personality.

Now if we want to integrate the neurotic personality, we first de-structure the symptoms. In other words, we do not try to get rid of the headaches or obsessions by annihilating them, by cutting them out. This would cripple the patient if it were possible; we leave such attempts to lobotomists. But we aim to reorganize, to de-structure and re—structure the personality. Invariably when we do so, we find considerable aggression that has been bound up either in self-control, self-punishing, even self-destruction. We find aggression that has been projected and appears as chronic fear of an impending catastrophe. We find destructive aggression in irritability, withdrawing, withholding. In short, we find a lot of "surplus" aggression. But to hold that this aggression as such is responsible for the pathological distortions, like Hitlerism or sadism, is like holding the sexual drive responsible for the perversions. It is not aggression, any more than sex, that is responsible for the neuroses, but the unfortunate organization of aggression that occurs in our institutions and families, especially in the inability to cope with

From Planned Psychotherapy to Gestalt Therapy

137

industrial progress and the inferno of urban living. We have neglected our organic discrimination and thus we have diminished the amount of satisfaction in our lives. Caught in rush and worry, we don't have the time to finish situations. Most of all, perhaps, instead of being attracted by what is interesting to them, people are driven by "duty," by the need to earn a living in occupations that are not appropriate to them, not true vocations, by greed for things instead of appetite for meaningful relations, by greed for entertainment instead of the effort for happiness.

In my opinion, all of this is importantly connected with the poor organization of our habits of eating; and in every therapy I devote considerable time to restructuring these habits. Disturbances of breathing produce symptoms of anxiety; disturbances of adequate and satisfactory intake of food produce, via the unemployed biological aggression, many neurotic troubles.

Let us collect our various threads.

The growth of the organism takes place by integrating our experiences, that is by assimilating to the organism the physical, emotional, and intellectual substances that the environment offers and that meet a need.

If no assimilation occurs, we are left with the introjects, the things swallowed whole, the foreign material that we have not made our own. Such is an introjected morality: it is the result of an incomplete aggression, an incomplete biting-off and chewing-up and digestion of the standards of parents, teachers, and society. Some of that food was perhaps not fit for the organism to begin with; it would never have been bitten off but was force-fed. This part must be vomited back. Other of it might have been potentially wholesome enough, but it was fed at the wrong time or in the wrong doses, so it was never digested. This part must be regurgitated, chewed through again, and digested.

From Planned Psychotherapy to Gestalt Therapy

138

Further, since the aggression was incomplete, since the organic de-structuring of the food was interrupted, there occurs a dissociation of part of the aggression into free-floating aggression; and the corresponding starvation recurs as greed. The essence of what is taken in by greed is that it does not satisfy; greed requires more and more to fill the bottomless pit — for the food does not nourish. On the plane of self-esteem, for example, if you are in need of praise, then no amount of praise you get will ever be enough, for the praise is not assimilated; it is deprecated (swallowed without savor) or becomes a source of boasting (vomiting it back). And the free-floating aggression, that should have been used for the assimilation, finds its way into tyranny, sadism, irritation, and so forth.

Encumbered by its introjection, the organism loses its proper discrimination; the stomach and mouth are sour or desensitized; there is no appetite. Then wrong choices are made, nourishment is looked for in the wrong direction, according to alien "needs." The result of this must be still further fixing of the habits of faulty and incomplete de-structuring, for without savor, appetite, and need, how can we expect a complete mobilization of the functions of aggression, whether toward food, sexual satisfaction, knowledge, or social relationships? Healthy aggression is nothing but applying oneself for the achievement of self-realization.

In therapy, on the contrary, step by step with restructuring the habits of aggression we examine and reevaluate the acts of discrimination. For example, with an exercise in chewing might come first gagging and vomiting, but then new sensations of taste and a more vigorous appetite. And, *vice versa*, with a reevaluation of what objects are disgusting and what objects have been sought out, might come first pains or cramps in the jaws and other muscles of aggression, but then a new strength to reach out for and bite off what is organically needful.

From Planned Psychotherapy to Gestalt Therapy

When appetite and aggression follow from the needs of the organism and the objects are discriminated by the organism, there is the security that was rigidly given by absolute moral standards. At the same time there is the flexibility and relativity necessary and delightful in the changing circumstances of the world, for there is no anxiety about losing the self: it is the self that is choosing.

In practice, of course, the greatest obstacle to reorganizing aggression is the patient's fear to hurt, or by retaliation, his fear of being hurt. Mostly, however, this fear to hurt can be shown to be nothing but self-deception and hypocrisy, for though he inhibits his action or scotomizes his wishes from hurting directly, he always hurts indirectly instead. He does it by showing the cold shoulder, by being late, by disappointing, by being in a bad humor, by being clumsy and breaking something, etc., etc., ad infinitum. It is not the conflict and the aggression brought to a conclusion, often to a creative and surprisingly satisfactory conclusion, that causes the misery, but the avoidance of bringing the fight into the open and clearing the air. Let me mention an extreme case, one of my patients in South Africa. He had lost a button off his jacket. For three weeks he felt acute resentment against his wife because she did not mend the button. But he did not speak to her about it, nor invest the five minutes necessary to mend the button himself. Instead he made himself and his wife miserable with his sulking for three weeks.

What is our conclusion with regard to morality and aggression?

The organism cannot tolerate an unfinished situation. With every finished situation, we feel good; with every unfinished situation, we feel bad. To finish a situation, in order to achieve well-being and stability, we mobilize our forces to attack the problem. The more obstacles that stand in the way, the more energies we are required to bring into play. In hunger, there is oral aggression;

wants and frustrations of other kinds involve other muscular aggressions. In language, when we feel good or are achieving the desired conclusion, our speech is soft and friendly; when we feel bad or are being frustrated, our voices grate and we curse. With regard to our fellows, when we feel good, we feel thankful, we have a sense of harmonious contact; when we feel bad, we attack in some way and try to change the environment. If we prevent ourselves from aggressing, we feel resentment or guilt instead.

So we must say: it is not aggression itself that is good or bad, but when we feel bad we feel aggressive.

From Planned Psychotherapy to Gestalt Therapy

Cooper Union Forum Lecture Series: "The Self"

"Finding Self Through Gestalt Therapy"

Fritz Perls delivered "Finding Self Through Gestalt Therapy" as part of the Cooper Union Forum Lecture Series: "The Self" in New York City on March 6, 1957. The talk includes many of the same ideas set forth in writing in "Psychiatry in a New Key." We have here a taste of Fritz — charming, boring, infuriating, and amazing an audience as he continued to do throughout his life. Fortunately, the talk was transcribed including the long pauses and the question and answer contact between Fritz and his audience.

Mr. Chairman, ladies and gentlemen: I see quite a number of people still coming in which reminds me of an old psychoanalytical saying "If you're too early, you're anxious; if you are on time, you are obsessional; and if you're late, you're hostile." So, I hear you jeering at this. Well, one can say, "Whatever you do is not right." Or one can just say, "Well, let's classify people in one of the three headings." In any case, I hope that the hostility of the late comers will not influence us too much.

From Planned Psychotherapy to Gestalt Therapy

You see, my friends tell me I am a very bad lecturer and a very good teacher. So, right now, I feel very, very confused. I don't know what to do, what to say to you, because I don't know what you want. I know what I want. I want to get something across, but what do you want? You see, this is my basic question. Whether I deal with a group, or with a patient, I think the basic idea is first to establish: what do you want? Now, what does a patient want from a therapist? A shoulder to cry on? Does he want somebody to confess to? Does he want a better memory? In any case he wants something. So, I wish I knew what you want.

You see, I don't think I can give you something through a lecture. I don't think words can convey anything, especially anything about Gestalt therapy. Maybe some of you know something about a peculiar philosophy, Zen Buddhism. If you know something about Zen, or even if you know something about General Semantics and the significances of the non-verbal level, I might be able to convey something to you. But in order to convey something, we first of all have to establish communication.

Now, communication takes place, like everything, in a "field." And the field is, like in modern physics, the basis of Gestalt therapy. We are here in a field. In this field there are a number of people, and there is me. It's a peculiar, let's say "Boundary" between me and you. Or as Buber, a famous Jewish existentialist, would say "between the 'I' and 'the thous'." This is, now, the essence of the 'self'." The self is that part of the field which is opposed to the otherness. You see, you can look for the self. Does the "self" exist? Does the "I" exist? Can you dissect the brain and find the "I," or the "superego," or the "self?" Definitely not. I think this is obvious. So what is this "self?" Now the "self" cannot be understood other than through the field, just like day cannot be understood other than by contrast with night. If there were eternal day, eternal lightness, not only would you not have the concept of a "day", you would not even have the awareness of a "day" because there is nothing to be aware of, there is no differentiation. So, the "self" is to be found in the contrast with the otherness. There is a boundary between the self and the other, and this boundary is the essence of psychology. Inside this boundary, this contact boundary where you and I meet, inside the boundary there are other disciplines: there is physiology, there is anatomy, and so on. And outside this boundary there is geography and sociology and so on. But psychology is exclusively interested in, and its place is exclusively, where the self and the other meet. Or, if you are outside the field, where a person and society clash, where an organism is embedded in its environment. Now this contact boundary, to be sure, is nothing rigid. It is something that is always, always moving. There is always something either coming into the foreground or receding. But we always meet. Whether I look at you and my eyes meet a "picture" that I can't see beyond, whether I hear, whether I feel and touch, always, where I meet the other there is the boundary. There is awareness. There is experience.

Now we come to the basis of our approach. Namely, we consider ourselves, as I consider myself right now, a part of the field. If I am with the field and experience myself and my reactions as part of the field, then I use myself as a tool of therapy. I get involved. I can get involved with the total field situation, which we call "sympathy." Or I can keep myself out and look at the patient only through the microscope; then I feel "empathy." Or I am not interested; then we call it "apathy." Who listens? There is nothing going on.

Now, what is going on in this field? What is the contact function of myself and the environment? Well, basically it is in the human being the idea of communication. Now what do we communicate and what do we want to communicate? Well, let us first look at the different stages of communication as applying to therapy. I

From Planned Psychotherapy to Gestalt Therapy

would say the first stage is non-communication. The patient doesn't know what he wants; he has nothing to communicate. Whatever he wants or needs, as they say in the Freudian jargon, is repressed. He is not aware of anything. So, after a while, I am aware of something in the patient. I see that you are playing with your hands, you are doing this . . . , you are kicking with your foot. In other words, I can already have some communication.

Rather, the patient, without knowing it, communicates something to me with his gesture language, often called "fidgeting." Now this fidgeting is the most important language with which the patient, at the non-communicative stage, tells us something:

> If he does this. . . . .he might tell us he wants to be stroked,
> If he does this. . . . . it means he probably wants to kick us, and
> If he does this. . . . . .it means "I am sad" or,
> if he does this. . . . . .it means "I could just bite you."

Now, from there, the state of non-communication develops into a state of inhibited communication. This means the patient feels something; he wants to cry; he has secrets but is ashamed to tell you this. This is the moment of the state of inhibition; he holds something in: *inhabile* (that cannot be handled or managed). And there you can always see the personal conflict: one part is turned against the other. We can then deal with this conflict and make clear to the patient that a part of him, which, for the time being, we call the "I" is turned against another part which we might call the "self." He is nagging himself, he is telling himself, he is punishing himself. And he is doing all kinds of things with himself, thereby encapsulating him. Instead of a contact boundary, which in the first state was completely missing, we have now a wall. Or, as Wilhelm

Reich used to call it, we have an "armor" between him and the world. I can deal with the armor in several ways. I am going to talk about it somewhat later. Let me first finish the development. Now, if the patient does not hold back anymore, we then get the third stage, the exhibitionistic state or random communication. This is the state which the Freudians, or the psychoanalysts in general, ore satisfied to achieve. In this state the patient exhibits his dreams, he exhibits his misery, his sins. He talks "about" himself. And I call it random communication because he puts, so to say, the cards on the table, waiting for somebody to pick up whatever he wants to. But this is not yet efficient communication.

The next state is the efficient communication, where you really express what you want, where the patient really makes contact with the therapist. And this is, again, in contrast to the psycho-analytical procedure which, as you know, derived a lot of its technique from Freud's own embarrassment. Freud was a person with tremendous difficulties in making contact. He was a brilliant writer but he couldn't go out, he couldn't meet people, he couldn't look at his patients. He complained they were staring at him. His whole neurosis was built upon avoidance of that anxiety which results out of a good contact.

Efficient communication is so important. You can feel an annoyance with your wife, but if you don't express it fully what happens? Well, you can hold it back. You can be on bad terms for weeks, days at least. But if you have it out, if you express "For Heaven's sake, let's have it out," even if you fight, even if you have a conflict which can't be solved, it is still better than "A certain person doesn't talk to me." You know all this kind of random communication we use to indulge in.

Right now I have nothing to communicate. (Long pause, with uneasy, random laughter from the audience)

From Planned Psychotherapy to Gestalt Therapy

147

Now, you see what I just did was a typical little piece of Gestalt therapy. I just expressed what I felt and through this expression I managed to go on, I reestablished contact. I felt a warm laughter. I felt that you were with me at this moment. I was able to finish this unpleasant situation, this bit of discomfort that I felt, and maybe you felt, when I became silent.

So, from there we come to the next important point of Gestalt Psychology and Gestalt therapy; namely, the importance of unfinished situations. You can believe in instincts. You can believe in two instincts, as the Freudians have it, or fourteen, as the Behaviorists want it, or you can believe in two million instincts, or unfinished situations, as I like to do. I believe that our organism is so complicated that every time something happens to it, is experienced by it, we are thrown out of balance and at each moment we have to regain this balance. The scientists call this state "homeostasis," this eternal attempt to regain our balance.

Now, in this disturbance of balance if something happens which, through something non-self, comes about then we have the unfinished situation. What does this mean? We have an urge, a simple urge. Let's say, "I'm hungry." I eat. Then the hunger situation is finished for the time being. But now let's assume something interferes. Something says, "Ah, this food is poisoned." Let's take the simple case of a paranoiac who thinks the food is poisoned, because he wants to poison everybody, so he believes his food is poisoned. This interrupts his need for food, his eating. So he stops. His hunger remains unsatisfied, and this is the only moment where we, in Gestalt therapy, relate ourselves and our patient to the past. Wherever we find an unfinished situation it means we are still carrying with us some business from the past which we have to finish. And if we don't do it, well, just think for a moment of the symptom of insomnia.

From Planned Psychotherapy to Gestalt Therapy

What is insomnia, other than the attempt to finish unfinished situations? Say you have a revenge which you haven't carried out, you want to "get even" with somebody. Somebody has hurt your self esteem. So you toss and turn until you finally hit on the idea, "Ah, this is what I would like to do to him." And then you get angry, not with the dog that is barking outside, but with the subject with whom you want to get angry. Then you can finish the situation either in reality or in fantasy. You might get enough emotional release to fall asleep and then you might have some dream wherein you actually finish him off. So, the need for finishing unfinished situations is another important item of Gestalt therapy.

The next point I would like to make is the Existential aspect. In Gestalt therapy we are Existentialists, in contrast to being moralists or symbolists. When you look into your relationships with people, into the relationship of yourself with yourself (or your "I" with your "self"), you find that you are always, always full of shoulds. "You should do this," "Don't do this," "This shouldn't be," "This isn't fair." In other words, you are always trying to change the world, to do something and, believing that good intentions are mere words of "you should," that these letters S-H-O-U-L-D would have an actual power of transforming reality.

In contrast to this we try to see what exists. And what does exist are contact functions that strive for creation, for creating situations in which you can complete your own vocation, in which you can be and experience. These situations are not achieved with "shoulds," but they are achieved with anxiety. And this is, I would say, perhaps my greatest difference with the psychoanalytical schools. To them anxiety and guilt are the "bugs" of the neuroses and they say you have to avoid creating anxiety in the patient.

This is exactly the issue about which we have to talk right now, the avoidance of anxiety. To be anxious is the basis of going forward, of becoming outgoing, of doing something. Now, what

From Planned Psychotherapy to Gestalt Therapy

happens if you are anxious to do something and you do not dare to take the peep into the unknown? You stifle your anxiousness, and out of this former state of anxiousness you are no longer anxious to do something but you develop, instead, a state of anxiety. And, in this state of anxiety, there is the choice of creation. Think of the actor and his stage fright, and you can see the two possibilities of anxiety. Either you create defenses, or you create outgoing experiences. O.K. You might be able to create a mess, a rumpus, a piece of art. Essentially, what you want is to create something new, something that is not routine. Because, if you are in a state of routine, and this is, what happens to most, or many of us, you are bored with life, life goes by, nothing is worthwhile, and once this tendency towards routine, towards living in a safe place has started our anxiety is then invested in defense mechanisms. We make sure that we have enough to eat tomorrow, we make sure that we get to our job in time, we make sure of this, we make sure of that. The more you make sure, the more insecure you become. Because you can't make sure, because the drive toward the world is there. The only state in which you can be absolutely sure is the catatonic state, where you are dead.

Now, this anxiety is based on the basic energy in us, of the basic being of the human organism, namely, to be excited. You can be either bored (or indifferent), or excited. The excitement is not always visible as excitement. The excitement can be blocked. Let's start from there. For example, it can happen, as it did right now to a number of you, that you block your excitement and your interest, and then you are bored. I saw a number of people just now yawning. So, let's interrupt this, at this moment, and do a little bit of Gestalt therapy, of Gestalt group therapy, in order to do something about the interest that is not here, in this field. May I please ask all of you, or those who want to play, to close your eyes and imagine you are leaving this room right now. Go, in fantasy, go outside, go

From Planned Psychotherapy to Gestalt Therapy

to wherever you like to go. I will call you back in a minute's time. (general laughter from the audience)

Silence. (little more than half a minute)

I see at least one lady who was very bored before, now happy and smiling. And, I hope that one or another of you has also, in the meantime experienced the essence of the unfinished situation. Maybe you went home or somewhere else, and tried to finish a situation which was unfinished which you still have to finish. All right, you did it only in fantasy and, if I have time enough, I might still talk about that. But I hope that you are now a little bit more excited, at least, that you can produce enough excitement to pay attention. Of course, if I have nothing to communicate you cannot possibly pay attention, you would rather go off to other places. Now, this excitement is not always there as excitement. You see, it changes. It changes mostly into emotions. Excitement, for instance, can manifest itself first as impatience, then as rage or anger. Or it turns out as sexual excitement and it can turn into affection and enthusiasm. Or the excitement of grief. There are all kinds of forms of emotions into which excitement turns. Now then, when this emotion is used by ourselves for creative purposes, the whole catharsis theory is rubbish. Nature is not so wasteful as to create emotions to throw them away.

Emotions are the very means of our ability to make contact. Even if I hit somebody, it might not be a pleasant contact, but, at least, it is contact. If I talk to somebody, it is contact, or potential contact. But contact is established only if it has the support of your feelings, of your convictions. A scientist who wants to talk to a scientific audience needs the support of his knowledge, of his interest, in conveying something to that audience. Now, anxiety is excitement minus oxygen. You get excited but you don't breathe, and because you don't breathe the heart action has to race, to bring more red blood particles to the different tissues of the organism. To

From Planned Psychotherapy to Gestalt Therapy

cope with a state of anxiety, breathe fully and, in fantasy at least, take the leap into the future, dare to do whatever you want to do. Not necessarily in reality, and then consider the alternative. "If I don't do the things I want to do, if I build, instead, defense mechanisms, if I am afraid, what happens then?"

By the way, as I want to conclude these thoughts on anxiety, know that breathing means exhaling. There is a fetish in our time about breathing, the big chest, the he-man fetish that thinks breathing is inhaling. But breathing means throwing out the bad air. You would not go to a basin and wash your hands with the water, dirty water, half full in the basin. And you don't pour clean water on top of it. Now the same with breathing. First get rid of the bad air, the carbon dioxide, and then bring in the fresh air. If you can do this, the acute state of anxiety, or asthma, will very quickly disappear. As a matter of fact, in asthma, you often see children forcefully exhaling, "Wwhueeeue . . ." "whueeeue . . ." Thus nature takes over. But the child is being told to "breathe." To him this means to inhale, and thus you create an artificial conflict in him. And the same applies to the orgasm, to the sexual situation. If you don't exhale fully you cannot have a full sexual experience.

Now, as to the other idea of psychoanalysis, guilt as one of the basis of neurosis. Let me give you a kind of short cut. I know how dangerous it is to give short cuts if you are not fully versed with the material. But I think this little short cut, let's call it a gimmick, I can use here; it can't do any harm.

It might, possible, ease the situation a bit. Especially in regard to guilt. It is a very, very simple gimmick which can help you when you feel terribly, terribly guilty and you do all kinds of things to atone and to pay for your debts and your guilt. It is the realization that guilt is nothing but reversed resentment. There are two expressions which you have to rediscover. One is "I feel so hurt." If you translate it and say, instead, "I feel so vindictive," "you are much nearer the mark. I can examine you to see where you feel hurt, or where your poor, poor mother is hurt when you come home late. If you examine where she is hurt, she isn't hurt anywhere, but she feels very mad at you. The same with guilt feelings. The other expression, "I should not have done it" can be translated, always, "You should not have done it." Also, instead of "I feel so guilty that I didn't do thus and so," say instead, "I feel resentful that you didn't do thus and so." You will be amazed how quickly you can sense that this is right, that it clicks, that these guilt "feelings" and the "feeling hurt" were merely hypocritical. They were not honest feelings, they were not genuine. (long pause).

How is the boredom? (another long pause)

I wish this was discussion time and you would ask me something, I would like to know what you want, whether you understood, whether I could make myself clearer, whether we have efficient communication or not. I wish I could elaborate on this point, or that point, but, apparently, I have to go on giving my monologue. (laughter) Well, let me ask something. (turns to Fairchild, the chairman).

Yah, I am not allowed yet to . . . (laughter)

Well, then, let me tell you something about my idea of a "no mind" organism. I don't believe that we have a "mind." This sounds very funny, I know. You see, I believe that we have, still, a mentality like the pre-Socratean naturalist. They thought the universe was made out of earth, water, air and fire. So, we believe we are made out of a body, and a soul, and a mind, and a libido, and on unconscious that is sandwiched between the mind and the body. And especially, there is always the "mind" that is looked upon as an entity, as opposed to the body, the "mind," where the associations are running along and pulling each other, as on a string, and somewhere these are connected with the body. I don't know. How? There are some vague theories of Freud about "psychological equi-

From Planned Psychotherapy to Gestalt Therapy

valent" but these are never made clear. Then there is another theory of a "psycho-physical parallelism," that whatever happens in the physical world happens, at the same time on the mental level, or vice-versa. Now, my idea is this, I think the difference between earth and water is not that of different entities but, rather, a difference of quantity. For example; ice, water steam and H_2O are different from each other merely by the quantity of temperature and density. Steam is existential, and H_2O is symbolic, a representation of the real thing. Something similar to this, I believe, is the case with us.

There is first the basis. Let us call it the "animal self." Here, we are like little children, merely organic beings with their needs, their primitive functions, though often very differentiated functions, and their feelings.

The next layer would be a diminished layer. I call this the "as if" layer, or the "social layer." In the social system the loss of nature is replaced by rules of games. Society always copies nature very badly, and the worse the copy, the imitation, the counterfeit, the easier it will be for a whole nation to perish. The closer the rules of society, the laws, come to the laws of nature, which cannot be violated without punishment, the more survival value that society will have. Let us imagine a society that says, "O. K., now let us play tennis, but if you go beyond this white line, that is a taboo, you violate the rules. If you violate the rules, and play beyond the white line, you will be punished by death." Of course, this is absurd and I think you realize that I deliberately exaggerated this example. But realize that whatever society is, and does, is an "as if" function. It is a game, a game unfortunately, which many people take damn seriously. And this game is played by different rules in different societies, primitive societies and higher societies. But what is always there is the game. And what is always there is a training in this game, a ritual of doing things together so that one is sure that ev-

From Planned Psychotherapy to Gestalt Therapy

erybody follows the same rules, so that we all "play cricket." You can see that this "as if" function is already less intense than the real function. If I pretend to be friendly, and assume a character, an appearance, then I don't invest as much of my energy as when I really mean to be friendly. The whole idea of character structure belongs to this "as if," this "social layer."

The next layer is the "fantasy layer," often called "mind." Please realize when we talk about "mind," in this context, we don't mean something opposed to the body. Rather, we mean something like the organism or the body, but in a very minute scale. It was Freud, really, who first pointed out the importance of this. Unfortunately, he lost it later on. He called the thinking process a "probe-handling," a "trial act." Now, this is actually what you have a fantasy, or a mind, for. Don't be dismayed by the word "fantasy," it does not mean that you have to be irrational. There is a rational fantasy and irrational fantasy, just as our actions can be rational or irrational. If you want to buy a piece of bread in a strange town it is very rational to start by imagining, "I could go this way, or in that other direction, where I saw those shops." In other words, you first buy in fantasy. As a matter of fact, in all the "making sure" business I spoke about in relation to anxiety, you find a tremendous amount of fantasy work involved.

You may have to see your bass the next morning so you start rehearsing, "What am I going to say to him?" "What is he going to say?" And so on. All the time you try to make sure, you imagine, you fantasize what will happen. Then you are amazed, because the one thing you forgot to rehearse will happen.

Now, the next layer would be covered by the isolation, or rarification, or "objectivation layer." Here you tear sounds and tools out of their context and make them ready for a new organization. For example, an ape has tools too. He takes a stick and gets a banana down. But he throws the stick away and the stick doesn't

From Planned Psychotherapy to Gestalt Therapy

exist anymore; it recedes in the background. But once we isolate this stick and make this stick a tool, always handy when we need it, then it becomes an object, not just a "means whereby," as before. The same with sounds. Take these original sounds, "aruah-gooah." If I use the word "aruah-gooah" often enough in connection with this then finally, "aruah-gooah" will be a means of communication, if I say this to somebody else, he will bring me this "aruah-gooah," or whatever it is. Of course, I cannot go into any greater detail into the whole question of the relationships of symbolism, and language. I suggest that you read Wittgenstein (*Tractatus Logico-Philosophicus* and the *Philosophical Investigations*) about it.

Now, the next stage, the final stage, is where we combine and organize these symbols and tools into machines and language. The essence of a healthy person is that there is a unity, an integration of all the layers; he does not live merely in one level. He does not use just "words," but his words do have feelings and visions and convey all the senses. Words are used as tools. The same with machines, with gadgets, and so on. In other words, by integrating all these five layers we become truly ourselves, which means, we can discover the other, the world. Because, this is the paradox: the more we have the other, the world, the more we can be ourselves. The more we lose the other, the more we become selfish and self-centered. And the more self-centered we become, again, paradoxically enough, the less we ore our real selves because, then, we are open to all kinds of intrusions from others.

QUESTIONS AND ANSWERS

Q: You ask, "What does the patient want to know, what does he want?" Well, I think I have an idea what some patients may want, and that is, they want their analyst or therapist to help them find themselves. Is that too big an order?

From Planned Psychotherapy to Gestalt Therapy

Perls: This is something, again, on which I could talk for a long while. You know the essence. Or, let's put it this way, there are many dichotomies blooming in today's psychiatry, and you know, they always have dichotomies, body and mind, infantilism and maturity, and so on. Now one of these dichotomies is this idea that there is such a thing as infantilism and maturity. If a child at an age of five years behaves like a child of three years, is this infantile or mature? You see how arbitrary this idea is. The fact is that we mature all the time, that our development, and this is the essence of growth, is from complete environmental support to a possible complete self-support. But, the child still needs a lot of support. He needs to be carried, he needs to be fed, as he gets older, he needs financial support, he has to be given emotional support, encouragement, and so on. Now the essence of the neurosis is that, the neurotic, instead of developing his own self support puts all his energy into manipulating the environment for support. For instance, a neurotic person cannot appreciate himself, so he tears himself to pieces to get the world to appreciate him. He has not enough self esteem, emotional self support. This is where "wanting" is of such great importance. It is so simple. We find out what does the patient want from the therapist and then, we see, this is the very thing he lacks, he needs. Here is the very attitude which remained undeveloped, unfinished in him. And then, rather than providing a goose chase into the past to see where did he transfer this unfinished situation from, and so on, and so on, we find out right now, what is he lacking? How can we develop this lacking appreciation as, for instance, in this case?

Now, when we find, for instance, that he is depreciating himself, nagging himself all the time, we take this nagging and direct it toward us. Here we find out that he actually wants to nag us, to get and squeeze some appreciation out of us. From this he learns to

From Planned Psychotherapy to Gestalt Therapy

appreciate his ability to nag and, so, he develops some confidence from there.

Q: I would like the doctor to explain, what is the real relation between the word "gestalt," which is "form," and therapy. And then there is another aspect of the word "gestalt," in philosophy, as used by Kant. I would like to know the difference between the philosophic and psychologic aspects of the word.

Chairman: Oh, I'd like to hear it. (laughter)

Perls: Wait. I think it will be more interesting to explain what the experience, or the essence of a gestalt, is rather than give a definition or its historical development. You see, we couldn't live if we would register all the millions of shapes and forms, which we encounter day by day, without bringing some order into them. And we bring order into them by inherent ability of any organism, the human as well as the animal organism, to form gestalts. Now, a gestalt is a cohesive "one" which you can't cut up into different ports. You can, for instance, tear a house down into bricks, into windows, and so on. And when you have all the rubble there, you can count them, but it's not a house anymore. Now, take a quite well known gestalt, a melody. A melody can be transposed so that each part, each note, is different from the one that was before, but the melody, the gestalt, is still the same. So, the word "gestalt" comes from the German word "gestalten." It means "form," to make a form, a comprehensive "one." You see, our time is very much inclined to analyze, to cut things up, to cut people up. Very much so. Which reminds me of a very typical thing about growth and this cutting up. An old teacher of anatomy always told me "Be very careful when you cut up a corpse. You see, in a living being the tissue grows again and the scar heals, but when you cut a corpse, it never grows together again." This is the essence of the gestalt, the comprehensive whole, the perspective.

From Planned Psychotherapy to Gestalt Therapy

And, if you are interested in the philosophical situation, let me tell you this much. The whole idea of semantics, the whole idea of meaning, cannot really be understood without the gestalt approach, because a meaning is the relation of a foreground figure to its background. This sounds very strange to people who don't know anything about gestalt. Let me give an example of what I mean. Here, far instance, in a typewriter is a certain letter. This letter ("l"), can be read as "el" or as "one," you remember. If you put it in one context, let's say the word soldier, then this letter ("l"), this symbol, gets the meaning of "el." If you type 34135 then this same symbol ("l") suddenly takes on the meaning of a number. If you use any word, let's take "king," and use it in the context of a card game, this word has a different meaning than if held against the background, let us say, of the Buckingham Palace. So whatever there is, the gestalt, which means the relationship of one part compared with a context, a larger unit, is what gives meaning. If you ask for our meaning in life it means we place ourselves in relation to the universe, If our background is one of religion then we get our meaning, from our behavior, according to our religion.

Q: Dr. Perls, I've been asked very frequently by my well intentioned friends, who find me in therapy. "Well, look, if all you have to do is to find out what happened to you long ago, won't you grow?"

I reply to them that it is more like an emotional retraining. Would you settle this little detail?

Perls: Well, you see, we have to look at how we, or originally our environment but essentially we take responsibility or how we interrupt our ongoing, our natural processes. We interrupt our processes, we interrupt ourselves by tensing, by avoiding, by running away, by deviating our attention, and so on. Now, if we understand this type of interruption and, instead of interrupting our-

From Planned Psychotherapy to Gestalt Therapy

selves, have the courage to interrupt our environment then we can take the choice whether we want to be polite and neurotic, or impolite and healthy. We can learn to become more outgoing in realizing that in interruption there is contact, and in non-interruption there is isolation and withdrawal from the world. Thus we come to taking up the interrupted development once again.

Q: Dr. Perls, you speak of a need to maintain a kind of, let's call it a kind of mental equilibrium, a homeostasis, if you will, or completion, as you put it. Perhaps now, can you tell me what is the reason for this, or the motivation or drive behind this need for closure or experience? And when you have completed that can you tell me of any empirical studies which will back up your statement, other than just clinical insights by gestaltists like yourself?

Perls: Well the question sounds very difficult, but actually it is very simple. Now, what happens if your organism is dehydrated? You know that, for survival, you need a certain amount of water in your organism. If it is dehydrated, you cannot think well, you cannot digest well, and so on. Just imagine we are living for ten days without water, in a hot desert. So you come across a gestalt in the environment, in the otherness, namely an oasis, the thing, that will attract your attention. Let us say you have a "minus" gallon of water in your system. To this "minus" gallon you add a "plus" gallon from the oasis, you put it into your system and you have a "plus minus," or zero, which is a balance. I call this, lately, a reaching of the "zero-need." I don't want to go into technical terms but the essence is that we have a lot of "zero balances" required for optimal functioning. Whether you take the acid/alkaline balance, whether you take the amount of calcium, of hormones, and so on, that the body requires, there is always an optimum of functioning. For instance, an optimum of functioning of temperature is around 97 degrees. If you have a body temperature of 47 degrees, you can't function very well. So, the unfinished situation here is a need for a warmth of 30 degrees. There is always the tendency toward the achieving of this "zero point." If you have a surplus, then you want to get rid of this surplus. If you have a "minus" you want to take in this "minus." Each breath is such a completion of an incomplete situation. Just try to stop breathing for three or four minutes and then see if you can realize what an unfinished situation is.

Q: Dr. Perls, you mentioned before an idea that you had called the "no-mind." I wonder if you could elaborate on this with reference to the many arguments raised about the existence of a mind, the existence of a spirit within the body as an entity from the body, or relating in some way but still an entity, and how this fits into, whether this is a kind of mechanistic naturalism. Also whether this "'as if'" that you talk about, this "game," also explains religion, philosophy, art, aesthetics, and how all this fits into Gestalt therapy?

Chairman: Can you do this in about 10 seconds, doctor? (laughter)

Perls: Yah, but I want to be polite, I do not subscribe to any mechanistic nor idealistic, let's call it, *weltanschauung* (world outlook). All these mechanisms, idealisms, or mentalisms, they are all obstructions of a total whole. If you take a single pencil, a yellow pencil, you cannot say this yellow is the pencil, you cannot say the wood is the pencil, and you cannot say the carbon is the pencil. All together, this something can be, or is, a potential pencil. But again, only in the writing situation. I can use this same pencil as a kind of lever.

So, any kneeling down to words, as words, as absolutes torn out of their contexts is without meaning. That is why I emphasized before that any idea you have, any word you use, can be understood only if it is related, and clearly related, to the context. Other-

From Planned Psychotherapy to Gestalt Therapy

wise, what you do is advertising, you tear things out of their context. You print just a few words, which are just the opposite of what the critic really meant, and you bluff your way through.

Q: Could you give us a little mare information about the therapeutic value of breathing, in Gestalt therapy? Is that the same as the Yoga system of breathing?

Perls: The answer is no. But, you see, this is a good moment just to mention something else, namely, how we deal with questions. People ask questions for many reasons. Mostly, they ask questions in order to embarrass people, and to avoid making a statement. Actually each question, and this is a wonderful thing, each question contains its own answer. Try to make a statement out of any question, like the last question. If the questioner had made a statement he might have said something like "I am interested in Jungian psychotherapy. I am, also interested in knowing how do you compare with this?" In other words, we are shifted from his inquiry of a certain interest which he has and which is worthwhile developing. You see, I don't think any answered question will give you anything for the simple reason that nobody can stand truth if it is told to him. Truth can be tolerated only if you discover it yourself because then, the pride of discovery makes the truth palatable.

Chairman: All right, here's a gentleman who will take a chance though. He is going to ask you a question anyway.

Q: I'm very grateful, Dr. Perls, for your kindness and your great wisdom. You said, in the beginning of your lecture, that if those among us who understood Gestalt could understand Zen . . . I've never been able to understand either and I wish to get a little help. I am very guilty of falling under your last castigation, but I take the guilt.

From Planned Psychotherapy to Gestalt Therapy

Perls: Could you please use the word "resentful" instead of "guilty," and then repeat your statement?

Q: I don't resent you, I resent myself, I hope that will satisfy you.

Perls: Na, it doesn't satisfy me. Except if you could tell me, in detail, how you resent yourself. I can't visualize that.

Chairman: Doctor, it would take too long, he just told me all he hates about himself. But he still wants to know something about Zen and the relationship with Gestalt therapy.

Perls: Well, I give you a Zen answer. If you were hanging on a tree, by your teeth, over an abyss, and your hands are full and your feet are tied, and somebody asks you "How do you want to be saved?" What would you do?

Chairman: I think we heard this story a little differently about two weeks ago, doctor. It was two men hanging together and one said to the other, "How will we save ourselves?"

Q: I have two questions, Dr. Perls. You spoke of sympathy, empathy, and apathy, as one being in emotional rapport with another, in being in intellectual communication with another, and being completely indifferent to another. You also mentioned, at one time, that you had nothing to say. And when the audience laughed you said that you felt they were in sympathy with you, that you felt a warmth of human feeling there. Now, is there any connection between that and when an obese gentleman falls on the ice and the audience laughs. Is that sympathy, empathy, or apathy?

Perls; This is *schoden freude* (pitiful joy). There are as many different kinds of laughter as there are of crying. You see, crying is not always grief. You can cry by being moved, you can cry for joy, you can cry for a loss, and so on. The same with laughter. I don't

From Planned Psychotherapy to Gestalt Therapy

agree with Nietzsche that to laugh is, always to be mischievous with good conscience. There are all possibilities, from a slight smile that is benevolent to the devilish laughter of a stage villain going "Ha, ha, ha, ha, (very raucous)." The ripple of laughter I experienced earlier, I experienced as something warm. Whether it was or not I cannot judge. I can only judge, and this is what I mean, by "my experiences," and this is the only thing I have to go by.

Q: You mentioned guilt, and my question relates to this concept of guilt. I understood from you that it is not what we think it is, in ordinary language, but it's some involved psychological, or psychiatric, process whereby it is actually reversed resentment. Well how about ordinary, everyday things that you can see in the criminal courts every day? For example, a man goes out and steals, he lives licentiously for weeks, comes home drunk, kills his wife or children. Isn't it normal, and natural, for him to feel a sense of guilt? Is there some reversed resentment there?

Perls: Yah. You see, if you read Dostoevsky, for instance, you notice that the more a person is a "saint," the more guilty he feels. And the more a person is a juvenile delinquent the less guilty he feels. I don't know whether you know this, that guilt is not related to doing, but to not doing, which means, actually, the resentment, that another can do it but that you cannot.

And . . .

Chairman: Not quite satisfied. He'd like to ask again.

Q: But I have spoken to clergymen, to priests, about that and they have told me where people have done real wrongs, they've killed, they've come back, and in their confessionals indicated tremendous guilt, where there was real guilt. I don't quite agree with you, doctor, if I may.

From Planned Psychotherapy to Gestalt Therapy

Perls: Well, I don't say that there isn't such a thing as a real guilt. I have been referring to our feeling of guilt. To the neurotic guilt, which is based essentially on thoughts, on feelings, on dreams, and so on. I don't say that a real debt, if you borrowed somewhere a thousand dollars, that this thousand dollars is not real. But if you imagined you borrowed a thousand dollars from somebody and then you go to this fellow and say, "I am so sorry I can't pay you back the thousand dollars, I feel so guilty about it." He doesn't quite understand what you are doing. In your example there may be a certain amount of guilt, but even there, there is a tremendous resentment, though in the form of projection. This is strictly for the psychiatrist. In other words, the resentment is projected. One feels that society resents one's deeds, and so on. In these cases it is not as simple as the ones I am talking about. I am referring to the every day "I feel guilty," "I shouldn't have done it," and so on. "I should have said this," instead of telling the other person, "You should have said this."

From Planned Psychotherapy to Gestalt Therapy

Gestalt Therapy and Cybernetics

In 1958, Jacob L. Moreno invited Frederick Perls to write an article discussing the similarities between Gestalt therapy and Cybernetics for publication in Moreno's publication, Sociometry: A Journal of Interpersonal Relations. (*Moreno decided not to publish the article.*)

Gestalt therapy has been in existence for only six years. In spite of its relative newness it shows a development out of proportion to such a short duration. It has attracted psychologists mainly, possibly on account of their appreciation of Gestalt psychology. But it has found few friends among psychiatrists, in spite of the fact that (except for some aspects of the Reichian and many of the behavioristic approach) it is more compatible with medicine and biology than any of the present methods of psychotherapy. A cerebral localization of the superego, for instance, has not even been attempted. The soundness of our approach is shown by the rapid improvement of our theoretical knowledge and by the simplification of our technique. This contrasts favorably with closed systems such as psychoanalysis.

From Planned Psychotherapy to Gestalt Therapy

It all came about with an observation apparently unimportant from the psychological point of view. Nearly twenty years ago, when I was still an orthodox analyst, I took into account the fact that we have two kinds of teeth with two different functions, the cutters and the grinders. The task of the grinders appeared to me to be the destroying of the structure, the de-structuring of food in preparation for its assimilation. This not only changed the role of aggression from an outward turned death instinct to a life supporting assignment, it also had far-reaching consequences in regard to Freud's basic outlook; namely, his tendency to take pathological phenomena as the basis of health. In this instance he stopped at introjection, leaving the bits (attitudes, memories) intact and undigested, thereby missing the important aspect of assimilation and growth. There are many more instances of this kind showing that he simply did not go far enough. By blocking his view toward the laws of integration (which he took for granted), Freud made his world-changing discoveries, but burdened himself and his followers with the Sisyphus task of the never-ending analysis.

Our assimilation idea led to the assumption that on the mental level memories are synthesized into Gestalten just as the stuff which is broken down in the healthy organism is synthesized into higher molecules. Memories disappear, except for unfinished situations incomplete Gestalten. (Imagine a waiter remembering all the orders he has ever taken! There is no need for a memory after the customer has paid his bill.)

Having rejected the total introjection of Freud's ideas and taking only what suited my appetite, I was free to dine at other tables, to assimilate any stuff that promised to contribute to a holistic theory in compliance with Whitehead's demand for coherence, consistency and applicability.

Useful material was supplied by many disciplines, but in this report on the progress of Gestalt therapy we want to show especially to what extent we benefitted from the assimilation of parts of a new science, cybernetics, which finds much in common in the behavior of organic and technical matter.

Psychologically we have taken little from the Association psychology. Free associations by themselves are to be considered a symptom of schizophrenia, where they are appropriately termed "flight of ideas," indicating a lack of concentration and inability to organize one's thoughts. We have accepted much more from Behaviorism, and of the many valuable contributions of Gestalt psychology we certainly have adopted the field concept, the figure-background formation and the idea of the complete and incomplete Gestalt. Consequently, homeostasis and development could satisfactorily be explained by the organism's necessity to complete all unfinished situations in the sequence of their survival importance.

From the philosophical point of view we are existentialists, especially in the sense of Husserl's phenomenology. We consider all metaphysical and metapsychological speculations, ours included, serve the need of the creating individual. However, we are not pure phenomenologists as we assume that the organism works as a whole, as a unit, a hypothesis which has led, for instance, to the resolving of the body / mind dichotomy and to a satisfactory theory of emotions (transformation theory). [i] Linguistically, we follow the usual procedure of being extremely skeptical of everything obvious, We examine semantically every term which is usually taken for granted. It was, for instance, the examination of such words as "consciousness" and "mind" which have been treated as realities even by prominent semanticists, that led us to a truly unified concept of the organism. [ii]

With regard to techniques, cybernetics with its concepts of feedback, oscillation, and most of all, communication, helps us to achieve a similar consistency with modern thinking. It has much to contribute to our efficiency as therapists.

From Planned Psychotherapy to Gestalt Therapy

Let us now come down from the summit of these highly condensed and abstract generalities to a somewhat more practical level, to the field in which we live. This "field" is differentiated into the organism and the environment, into the "I" and the "You," into the "Self" and the "Other" (for the "Self" has no substance in itself), into individual and society. In this "field" psychology has its proper and well-defined place. This place is the ever-changing contact boundary between the individual and its environment. There experience takes place. There is excitement, creativeness, communication. What is inside this contact boundary belongs to the disciplines of physiology and anatomy, what is outside has to do with geography, sociology, etc., etc.

In the healthy person the contact boundary is well experienced and defined, though differently for each instance and individual. Just as the law requires you to be able to distinguish between "Mine" and "Thine," so the healthy person knows what is "I" and what is "Thou." The neurotic (and much more the psychotic) has mostly illusions about these boundaries. Their boundaries are either hazy and undefined, or else run right through the individual or the environment, or both, A striking example is the well-known phenomenon of a stern conscience: if it is internalized the communication goes on intra-organismically, if it is projected, one becomes defensive against the imagined discriminator who actually might be morally indifferent. The haze of the boundary may be characterized by the phenomenon of embarrassment which makes any contact wobbly and communication unprecise and ineffective.

True contact is based upon an appreciation of differences, upon the readiness to agree to disagree, upon the ability to respect the other's feelings and actions. With parents one often finds the opposite of contact with their children. They are in confluence with them. They do not appreciate the child's needs and individuality, but expect him to comply with their own wishes completely. Frustrated confluence easily turns into isolation and hostility. This isolation must not be confused with withdrawal, which (contrary to the usual belief) is in itself a healthy and necessary phenomenon except for certain extreme cases. (More of this later when we shall discuss the cybernetic rhythm of contact and withdrawal.) Isolation is directed against the environment: it is armor, defense, shutting off. Withdrawal is directed toward something, essentially towards a position of self-support.

Contact cannot be made without something supporting it. The better the support, the more efficient the contact. To get somewhere you need the support of your legs. Motorically, our undercarriage serves more for support, and the upper part, mainly hands, mouth, eyes and ears, serves more the functions of contact. Good manners support social contact; a knowledge of words, grasp of his subject, the ability to formulate well will bring the writer or speaker in good contact with his audience, Inadequate, unrealistic, inefficient contact with his environment is the very essence of each neurosis, and this is due in each and every case to underdeveloped or interrupted self-support. Being unable to cope with life the neurotic manipulates his environment to give him the needed support, to give him love, money, directions, decision, etc. The task of therapy is thus to change the tremendous amount of energy which he invests in manipulating the environment into making him self-supportive — not necessarily self-sufficient, as this is often a symptom of the lack of contact (e.g., masturbation).

Life is a continuous development from environmental to self-support. There is a long road from the baby's utter helplessness to the financial and emotional self-support of the adult. In vital situations where environmental support is no more forthcoming and self-support not yet established, we have an existential crisis. If the individual survives the catastrophe, he will make sure that such a dilemma will not recur. Such an existential trauma is far more per-

From Planned Psychotherapy to Gestalt Therapy

vasive than a sexual or self-esteem trauma. It should be clearly understood, however, that no more unearthing of any childhood trauma will ever cure any neurosis. This has to be done in the here and now by reorganizing the structure and functions of our patients. This has to be done by changing neurotic regression and manipulation into a healthy rhythm of contact and withdrawal.

Instead the term of "withdrawal" we can reformulate and say: to alternate the contact with the environment and with one's own resources, For instance: I lack a relevant word during a conversation and I withdraw my attention for a fraction of a second to search in my memory for a suitable expression (in the meantime, filling the external gap with ah-ah-ah) and return to the conversation with the required word.

The alternation, shuttling, oscillation between contact and withdrawal, provides us with the model we need to appreciate the cybernetic approach to psychotherapy, We need this approach for the simplification of our endeavor to reintegrate the dissociated neurotic personality.

We know from physiology that a muscle reacts only to the opening and closing (contact and withdrawal) of an electrical circuit. We achieve a prolonged contraction of the muscle by using an alternating current (instead of a galvanic one) which provides the series of stimulations we need. Something similar applies to the working of the total organism. Here the efficiency and integration of dichotomized parts is accomplished by balancing them through proper steering. If you learn to ride a bicycle you will first, in order to maintain your balance, oversteer it to the right and to the left. Each time you overshoot, you will correct your mistake by a negative "feedback" that again will bring you too far to the other side. As time progresses you will become more and more subtle in your overshooting until you are no longer aware of the steering effort. But, no matter how expert you become, any bicycle which is so

From Planned Psychotherapy to Gestalt Therapy

constructed that you cannot move the handle beyond the middle line to the right or left will become impossible for riding.

Freud's shuttling between a dream and its background (association), Moreno's alternating play of the patient and his opponents, show the practicability of the cybernetic approach. But its scope is much larger. We have to learn to shuttle between many more areas such as

- the part and the whole,
- the foreground figure and its background,
- the I and the You,
- the memory and the present (sensations and emotions),
- the present and the future,
- the ecteroceptive nerves (medium of object-awareness) and the
- proprioceptive nerves (self-awareness).

Our limited space does not allow us to go into extensive discussion of those different areas, nor does it allow us to deal with other cybernetic terms like "scanning" and the "all-or-nothing" principle; but in order to illustrate the three cybernetic points mentioned previously (oscillation, feedback, communication), let us take the example of a hunter. He is not interested in random communication (which we will meet again as the third stage of therapy, the exhibitionistic phase); he is not interested in just shooting somewhere vaguely hoping to hit his prey. He wants efficient communication; he wants his bullet to hit the target. So he alternates between watching the deer and coordinating his muscles. The more the target moves, the more the hunter has to feed back the image to his motoric system and correct his aim. Of course, the trained hunter deals with minute fractions of a second. (But then,

From Planned Psychotherapy to Gestalt Therapy

Nachmanson has shown that the intraneural connections have a speed nearing a millionth of a second.)

In the neurosis such cybernetic processes are interrupted. It is the interruption of the ongoing processes which link the neurosis to medicine. Any interruption of an essential biological process "is" illness. The same designation applies to neurosis. Neurosis "is" the interruption of wholesome functioning, for instance, of behavior, communication, and Gestalt formation. The term "therapy" has the same meaning in psychiatry as in general medicine, namely the elimination of the interruptive agents or functions.

At last we can now visualize a therapy that operates with the precision of a surgeon. This comparison is not very valid, as we always tend to save and reorganize those energies which are invested in symptoms and resistances. It might nevertheless help us to clarify the requirements of an efficient psychotherapy.

The surgeon operates in the here and now on a patient who is present. He takes into account his own skill as he does the situation of the patient. Only instead of the one shooting operation of the hunter, he has to make hundreds of little operations (cuts, clippings, knottings, etc.) where again each single operation is cybernatically connected with (related to) the total operation. The surgeon also operates always on the surface. He has to deal with layer after layer. This means that after one layer has been dealt with, the next becomes surface.

The approach of Gestalt therapy is similar. Its simplicity, but also its difficulty, lies in the fact that we deal only with the present, with awareness and with the utmost surface (which, appearing as the obvious, is often neglected to the detriment of the treatment). The ideal therapy, that is, a maximum efficiency within the shortest time, should be like a good operation, It should be restricted to the here and now and the communication between therapist and patient. By restriction we do not mean exclusion of anything happening, but we mean that everything should and can be related to the here and now communication or the lack of it. If a patient complains about his wife, you can ask him: *"What are you telling this to me for?"* or *"What has this to do with me?"* If he answers, *"I want you to appreciate my troubles,"* he has expressed directly what he wants from you. He has not yet told how your appreciation of his troubles will give him support nor why he needs that specific kind of support, but he has taken a step toward it.

Vaguely we can classify four stages of communication, Though all four stages can appear in one session, the overall picture of a good therapy should show a development from the first to the fourth kind.

a) **Non-communication.** This phase stretches from a catatonic state to the sentence games you hear, for instance, at cocktail parties where any relevant conversation is nearly taboo. During the therapeutic session the patient may withdraw into a trance, he may report that he has a blank, or he may fill the gap of a sentence with "ah-ah." This gap contains for us some bit of non-communication, In Gestalt therapy we are doing microscopic psychiatry. We find the cues and levers for the change of our patient in the most minute details of his behavior. At the first stage, he is not aware of many areas of confusion or anxiety. He might be aware of a symptom but not of its communication value. He might feel a pain in the neck, but he is not aware that he thinks the therapist is "a pain in the neck."

b) **Inhibited communication.** The patient is aware of his censoring or avoiding of topics or experiences of emotions. But he does not express his *"I don't want to."* This is the period where self-control, politeness, not-want-to-hurt-you is glorified. The anti-self (ego-ideal, self-esteem system, overcompensation) domi-

From Planned Psychotherapy to Gestalt Therapy

nates the situation. There is a lot of intraorganismic communication (thinking, inner conflicts, indecisiveness) going on.

c) **Random communication**. Inhibitionism turns into exhibitionism. The patient exhibits his misery, sins, dreams, or what
have you, hoping the therapist will pick up what he is interested in, hoping for pity, absolution, interpretations, or whatever environmental support is needed.

d) **Efficient communication**. The patient expresses his needs and
emotions. Extremes of efficient one-way communication are
hypnosis and military drill; of inefficient communication, the
alcoholic's resolution to stop drinking.

Again it was Freud who first recognized the importance of
communication, of relating all the material available. And again, as
in the case of assimilation, he stopped short of the integrative functions. He was satisfied with the third (exhibitionistic) stage, with
the patient talking "about" himself or things. He even discouraged
personal contact. But good contact is impossible without adequate
self-expression which requires the full support of an uninterrupted
transformation from excitement to emotion to action.

Communication is, of course, a two-way affair. Technically
speaking, the signal does not come through if there is too much
background noise, thus the figure cannot stand out in relief. Our
patients do not get our messages for many possible reasons. Perhaps they have had to develop a mental hard-of-hearing attitude to
protect themselves against someone else's jabbering or nagging,
and still live in the acoustic ivory tower. Or else, they are twisters,
misunderstanding to suit their purpose. You ask them, *"What do
you feel?"* and they answer with what they think. Sometimes one
has to repeat such a question at least a dozen times, possibly inter-
spersed with the "did-you-get-my-message" question, until they can
duplicate, that is accept. the message.

From Planned Psychotherapy to Gestalt Therapy

Nothing blocks contact as much as uncommunicated emotion. An unexpressed grudge might lead to a cold shoulder treatment lasting for weeks. In group therapy, if I notice a dragging or a tedious atmosphere, I ask each group member to formulate his feelings about the atmosphere and I have still to come across a time when this simple procedure failed to mobilize the group into relevant and lively activity.

Although we use a feedback technique that, on the surface, resembles Roger's client-centered therapy, there is a fundamental difference. Instead of reformulating the patient's sentences, thus doing some clarification work for him, we are very careful to use only his exact words and images (including the most trivial metaphors in a literal sense). In *"Where do we go from here?"* or *"A thought struck me,"* we point to the moving or violence as intrusion of this fantasy life into the verbal, thus facilitating the exploration of his fantasy behavior; for what basically is wrong with the neurotic is his inability to make his imagination an integral part of his total functioning.

How do we open up the neurotic's creative imagination and keep it in harmony with rationality?

The grammar of effective communication is the order, the imperative, the expressed demand. This includes the question, which is a demand for information. First the patient has to learn to express his demands openly and with full feeling. *"Help me." "Let me do it by myself." "Leave me alone." "Stay with me." "Give me a magic pill." "Love me." "Admire me." "Drop dead." "Jump in the lake."* Though this is still manipulating the environment for support, it is now done with full awareness.

The trouble with the imperative is that it is only concerned with the end link of a chain, with the "goal," and this is often hazy. We mobilize the patient's creative imagination by persistent "How's": "How shall I admire you?" "How shall I jump into the

From Planned Psychotherapy to Gestalt Therapy

lake?"; he fills in the gaps, overcomes his helplessness, assimilates his projections, etc., etc, In other words, he learns to stand on his own feet — learns to organize his life to his satisfaction on a rational basis. Instead of approaching life with rigid and unidirectional alternating with omnipotent and perfectionistic ideas, he opens up the vista of "possibilities," And this, as Kierkegaard, a pioneer existentialist, said, is the "way out of despair."

i   The excitability of the protoplasm is experienced as (1] unspecific excitement. the quantity of which is produced by the organism according to the requirement of the situation. It is then (2) transformed into moods and emotions. The now qualitative (hormonal) change is felt as sexual excitement. grief. rage. fear. disgust. etc. In the course of this transformation the basic excitement loses its general vagueness more and more and appears as total involvement in a specific direction. The emotion then (3) is transformed into its specific and useful activity. It is not discharged. Nature is not wasteful. as the adherents of the cathartic theory would like to have it. Rage assumes the joyful character of fighting; grief. the mellow consolation of crying; sex. the ecstasy of the orgasm; fear. the motoric activity of running. etc. Examples; interruption of (1) produces anxiety. of (2) projections. of (3) psychosomatic symptoms.

ii   Most often the concept of the human organism still has the primitive outlook of the pre-Socratic naturalists. They thought the universe was made up of four substances: Earth. Water. Air and Fire. Compare this to the later idea that the same substances can have different forms through the mere difference of density and temperature. like Ice. Water. and Stearn (and we may add their symbolic representative H_2O). Today many psychiatrists practically treat the human organism as being composed of a Body and a Mind with the Unconscious sandwiched between them and dynamically held together by a substance called Libido. (Science has long debunked the notion of the "Soul" as a separate entity. though we have retained its poetic use. We should do the same

From Planned Psychotherapy to Gestalt Therapy

with the "Mind" and "Consciousness" which denote fantasy. deliberateness. attention. awareness. and what not.) A unified concept (comparable to what we said before about water) would have at least five stages of intensity:

(1)   The totally involved person (the Self).

(2)   The "as if' activities (playing and play-acting. deliberate character assumptions and pretenses)

(3)   The fantasy level. which can. like the actual level. be rational or irrational (Freud's *Probehandlung*. rehearsing. anticipating. recalling. thinking. which is fantasy speech to oneself or a person known or unknown. planning. day or night dreaming. and all kinds of activity involving still less energy expense than (2).

Man and the animal world share stages (1) through (3). e.g. Cubs play "as if' they were biting each other. the conditioned dog reacts "as if' the bell represents food. (3) Kechler has shown the execution of an imagined solution by chimpanzees; Masserman. the "acting out" of a fantasy in a monkey.

(4)   Level of isolation — The decisive break with the animal world occurs through the creating of 'objects' by tearing ports out of a context. Tools remain ready for use. They are not merely produced for a situation and discarded. Sounds are made into symbols no longer requiring the presence of an object or even its imagination.

(5)   The concepts level. where tools become machines and symbols language.

The interruption of the coherence and interrelation of any of these levels (compartmentalization. dissociation. mal-coordination. dichotomy) leads to neurosis and many types of psychosis. Health is the optimal coordination of all levels.

From Planned Psychotherapy to Gestalt Therapy

Resolution

This paper was given as a talk at Mendocino State Hospital, Talmage, California in 1959 as the conclusion of a series of talks and demonstrations by Perls.

In our lectures and demonstrations I have presented Gestalt therapy as a series of bits and pieces which you may find of use. I assume now that you know much and I can go beyond the categories, divisions, and pieces to explore the center point, the resolution of the closed gestalt. My ambition has been to create a unified field theory in psychology. In this lecture I would lead you from the play of opposites to the unity of resolution, so that you might experience the goal implied in Gestalt work. This is the other side of the coin: unity instead of division; resolution, a coming home instead of wandering. As in all things the main barrier to resolution is ourselves, and particularly how we fantasize about ourselves and the world. In many respects resolution can seem so pleasant, mild and simple that we distrust it and by our questioning undo its peacefulness.

From Planned Psychotherapy to Gestalt Therapy

It is said we *have a mind*, that we *have an* id, ego, and so on. By projecting living experience into external categories we fantasy that we have grasped and can control something. I propose the idea of universal awareness as a useful hypothesis that runs counter to this tending to treat ourselves as things. We *are awareness* rather than *have* awareness. From our aware experiencing we can look on the rest of existence and suppose that there are varying degrees of awareness in all things. The flower that turns to the sun is aware of sunlight. The rock that falls experiences some difference between falling, hitting and lying still. In varying degrees, all things which are *this* rather than *that*, function *this* way rather than *that, are* varying degrees of awareness.

Awareness, consciousness, or excitement are similar experiences. Man's awareness appears more comprehensive and hence more ambiguous than that of other things. The rock can only fall when it has no support: Without support we can project, repress, desensitize, etc. With the hypothesis of universal awareness we open up to considering ourselves in a living way rather than in the aboutisms of having a mind, ego, superego and so forth. Also, by the hypothesis of universal awareness we open up to considering ourselves as intrinsically like the rest of existence. Starting from *isness*, this awareness here now, *we* consider ourselves as we are, living, here, varied and similar to others and the rest of existence. It puts us in a position to contact, to move over boundaries, to range across differences, to find resolution.

Whether our awareness is greater than or more intense than that of animals, bacteria, cells, plants or stars I do not know. We need to suspect the vanity of saying we are the most conscious. It seems clear, though, that our awareness is the most ambiguous. It seems to split, divide and conceal itself more easily than rocks and plants. Most of what we have talked about is this apparent tendency to divide into foreground (what we sharply experience) and

From Planned Psychotherapy to Gestalt Therapy

background (what is less differentiated). Foreground is in dynamic relationship to background. Very simply, *what cannot be here, is there*. Background is all other; the world outside, meanings projected, other selves as dreams, our potentials, everyone and everything else. What cannot be here, is anyway and so is there; or, at least, *appears there*. If I cannot leave the room when I feel like it, I leave in fantasy. That way I can be here and there simultaneously. I can be kind and unkind, elated and depressed and so forth, simultaneously. It is partly the assumption that "I am this and not that" which is wrong, which creates a division, which we will need to amplify so that the missing part can also be conscious.

Actually our idea of the unconscious as being what is packed away and unused is wrong. What we do not know as ourselves is lived out anyway and can be seen by friends. It is as if we have a conservation of mental energy that corresponds to the conservation of matter/energy in Einstein's relativity theory. Nothing ever dies or disappears altogether in the realm of awareness. What is not lived here as consciousness lives there as muscle tension, unaccountable emotion, perception of others, and so forth. Nothing disappears, but much is displaced or misplaced. Boredom, for instance, which is a dreary state, also contains a drive to do something. The man dying of thirst has water everywhere except on his tongue. In Gestalt therapy we are in the paradoxical situation of always dealing with a two-part existence, what is awareness here and now, and what this awareness stands in relation to. Foreground implies background. The background shapes foreground.

What cannot come forth here appears there as other. My rejected resentment turns up as your obvious faults. Most of therapy is finding these splits, and activating both sides. Any activating of both sides tends to gather them together again. Questions are created out of the suspicion of the answer. The question that is intensified collapses into its own answer.

From Planned Psychotherapy to Gestalt Therapy

183

It is partly the demand for differences, the questioning, that divides. What are you aware of now? This rather than that. Can you be aware of this and that? Well yes, but not with the same intensity. The demand for intensity, the questioning, the expecting of this rather than that, creates the foreground-background misplacing of part of ourselves.

In love and especially in orgasm it is as though we experience across the boundary of selves to a contact that leads to the confluence of orgasm, to unifying differences. Understanding, which is more than aboutism or bullshit, is also an assimilation of differences. But let us for the moment break out of the differences which our concepts, our psychopathologies, and our ways of thinking almost insist upon, and join in universal awareness, in the zero point of creative indifference, the resolution of the quiet center.

In Taoism there is the yin/yang symbol which represents the interplay of opposites. The white half of the circle is growing darker, and the dark half is growing whiter. The two interact to make the round of existence. What is it like to experience both sides at once? It is ambiguous. "Am I a strong heterosexual man or an effeminate homosexual?" A full awareness can experience both, and not need to resolve the difference. "Do I love or resent her?" I can experience both and this brings life and complexity to our relationship. Emerson said consistency is the hobgoblin of small minds. Consistency demands that we experience one or the other. Much of the time we experience both sides, opposites. And this enriches the range of our possibilities.

In fact, the more you try to be just one-sided, the more the other side is also experienced. If I must be strong and dominant in all situations, I am forever watching for and experiencing potential weakness. If I must be a very good saint, I become aware of evil everywhere. If I am good, you appear evil. We don't hate or love the world, only ourselves. Each is the all of awareness. Resolution

From Planned Psychotherapy to Gestalt Therapy

is closer to experiencing good and evil, dominance and submission, top-dog and underdog. The more we would tilt all power to top-dog, the more powerful underdog becomes. It is the effort to make a top-dog which creates the equally powerful underdog. At the point of resolution top-dog and underdog are both present aspects of the same dog. You can enjoy the yin or the yang of opposites in this Chinese symbol, or experience it as a unified balance, which we call, simply, awareness. As the yin and yang interplay our consciousness is rich, varied, changing, exciting, not quite predictable, surprising.

Although we are dealing with the resolution of conflict, to find the satisfied and somewhat ambiguous center between opposites, I would also like to resolve our conflict with conflict. Suppose, for the moment, we could satisfy everyone's needs fully — a world of satisfaction. Would all action stop? Perhaps people would sit and sleep for a day or two, but action would begin again. Here a man would choose to build a needed workshop. A woman would make a dress, and so on. Out of this renewed action would appear again conflict, frustration, and difficulty. Though we need resolution for a time, just as sleep makes up one third of life, still it would be boring without action and conflict. Though we seem forever trying to put out the fire of conflict, we do not really want to put it out altogether. Perhaps we just want to contain it, like a fire in the hearth. If we didn't get thirsty we would fail to drink. But drinking enough is very different from drowning. Conflict, the unfinished situation, is itself a call toward resolution. The conflict we seek and respect is that arising out of the new combination of circumstances in the now. It is not an unaccountable replay reflecting what we dread and experience repeatedly. Therapy gets the individual past the dead replay to the new creative conflict which invites growth, change, excitement, the adventure of living.

From Planned Psychotherapy to Gestalt Therapy

There is but awareness endlessly coming forth. Beyond awareness there is nothing. At all points of discomfort it seeks to make
itself comfortable. This one awareness appears to split into
self/other so that in the trouble of search and finding, it can recall
its parts and find itself intensely. Unquestioned, in peace, it finds
itself as one. The apparent boundaries of me/you, mine/thine,
become fluid, disappear and reappear carelessly. It is not wrong to
question and divide, but it is even more complete to see that the
question arises from its own answer and that the function of
boundary and difference is to excite a contact resolution. The gestalt opens to demand closing and the energy toward closing is in
the opening.

The unified field is satisfaction, the oneness of what is, *isness*.
Question that this is so, and you create the split, the search, the
apparent need that could again lead to unity, satisfaction, the closed
gestalt. Deepen the split and it reaches across to find itself.

One symbol for this is the Buddhist *mudra* in which the thumb
and one finger make a circle. Thumb and finger appear as two,
making a circle, the round of existence. Yet these two are one hand,
one life. The other three fingers represent the multiplicity of existence which is also one hand and one life. In most gestalt work we
find and exercise the split, so that the parts of unity may come together. Yet, away from our own questioning and demands we can
enjoy the unity of awareness in which the division within self disappears as do the splits between self and others, self and the rest of
the world. One awareness. It is aware aliveness, experiencing conflict at all points that parts of itself have been displaced and growth
is called for.

Somehow I feel mellower than usual today. This is a fitting
place to end a series of talks. You have been a very receptive group
and I have done quite well.

From Planned Psychotherapy to Gestalt Therapy

Gestalt Therapy
and Human Potentialities

Reprinted from Explorations in Human Potentialities, *edited by Herbert A. Otto, Ch. 35. 1966. Charles C. Thomas, Springfield, Ill.*

Gestalt therapy is one of the rebellious, humanistic, existential forces in psychology which seeks to stem the avalanche of self-defeating, self-destructive forces among some members of our society. It is "existential" in a broad sense. All schools of existentialism emphasize direct experience, but most of them have some conceptual framework: Kierkegaard had his Protestant theology; Buber his Judaism; Sartre his communism; and Binswanger his psychoanalysis. Gestalt therapy is fully ontological in that it recognizes both conceptual activity and the biological formation of *Gestalten*. It is thus self-supporting and truly experiential.

Our aim as therapists is to increase human potential through the process of integration. We do this by supporting the individual's genuine interests, desires and needs.

From Planned Psychotherapy to Gestalt Therapy

Many of the individual's needs contend with those of society. Competitiveness, need for control, demands for perfection, and immaturity are characteristic of our current culture. Out of this background emerge both the curse and the cause of our neurotic social behavior. In such a context no psychotherapy can be successful; no unsatisfactory marriage can be improved. But, more importantly, the individual is unable to dissolve his own inner conflicts and to achieve integration.

Conflicts extend to the external as well. In demanding identification and submission to a self-image, society's neurotic expectations further dissociate the individual from his own nature. The first and last problem for the individual is to integrate within and yet be accepted by society.

Society demands conformity through education; it emphasizes and rewards development of the individual's intellect. In my language I call the intellect a "built-in computer." Each culture and the individuals composing it have created certain concepts and images of ideal social behavior, or how the individual "should" function within its framework of reference. In order to be accepted by society, the individual responds with a sum of fixed responses. He arrives at these responses by "computing" what he considers to be the appropriate reaction. In order to comply with the "should" demands of society, the individual learns to disregard his own feelings, desires and emotions. He, too, then dissociates himself from being a part of nature.

Paradoxically, the more society demands that the individual live up to its concepts and ideas, the less efficiently can the individual function. This basic conflict between the demands of society and one's inner nature results in tremendous expenditures of energy. It is well known that the individual ordinarily uses only ten to twenty-five percent of his potential. However, in times of emergency, it is possible for the conditioned responses to collapse. Integration becomes spontaneous. In such situations the individual is able to cope directly with obstacles and, at times, achieve heroic results. Gestalt therapy seeks to bring about integration without the urgency of emergency situations.

The more the character relies on ready-made concepts, fixed forms of behavior and "computing," the less able is he to use his senses and intuition. When the individual attempts to live according to preconceived ideas of what the world "should" be like, he brackets off his own feelings and needs. The result of this alienation from one's senses is the blocking off of his potential and the distortion of his perspective.

The critical point during any development, both collectively and individually, is the ability to differentiate between self-actualization and the actualization of a concept. Expectations are products of our fantasy. The greater the discrepancy between what one can be through one's inborn potential and the superimposed, idealistic concepts, the greater the strain and the likelihood of failure. I give a ridiculously exaggerated example. An elephant wants to be a rose bush; a rose bush wants to be an elephant. Until each resigns to being what they are, both will lead unhappy lives of inferiority. The self-actualizer expects the possible. The one who wants to actualize a concept attempts the impossible.

In responding to "should" demands, the individual plays a role not supported by genuine needs. He becomes both phony and phobic. He shies away from seeing his limitations and plays roles unsupported by his potential. By seeking cues for behavior from the outside, he "computes" and responds with reactions not basically his own. He constructs an imaginary ideal of how he "should" be and not how he actually is.

The concept of perfection is such an ideal. In responding, the individual develops a phony facade to impress others what a good boy he is. Demands for perfection limit the individual's ability to

From Planned Psychotherapy to Gestalt Therapy

function within himself, in the therapeutic situation, in marriage as well as other social situations.

One can observe in marital difficulties that either one or both of the marriage partners are not in love with the spouse but with an image of perfection. Inevitably, the partner falls short of those expectations. The mutual frustration of not finding perfection results in tension and increased hostility which results in a permanent status quo, an impasse or, at best, a useless divorce. The same condition applies to the therapeutic situation. Either a status quo of many years or a change of therapists occurs, but never a cure.

By turning his perfectionistic demands toward himself, the neurotic tears himself to pieces in order to live up to his unrealistic ideal. Though perfection is generally labeled an "ideal," it is actually a cheap curse which punishes and tortures both the self and others for not living up to an impossible goal.

At least two more phenomena interfere with the development of man's genuine potential. One is the formation of character. The individual then can act only with a limited, fixed set of responses. The other is the phobic attitude which is far more widespread than psychiatry has been willing to recognize thus far.

Freud was the genius of half-truths. His investigations of repression, blocks and inhibitions reveal his own phobic attitude concerning phobias. Once an impulse becomes dangerous, we turn, according to Freud, actively against it and put a *cordon sanitaire* around it. Wilhelm Reich made this attitude still more explicit in his armor theory. But danger is not always aggressively neutralized. More often we avoid and flee from it. Thus, by avoiding the means and ways of avoidance, we miss half the tools for a cure.

The organism avoids actual pains. The neurotic avoids imaginary hurts such as unpleasant emotions. He also avoids taking reasonable risks. Both interfere with any chance of maturation.

From Planned Psychotherapy to Gestalt Therapy

Consequently, in Gestalt therapy we draw the patient's attention to his avoidance of any unpleasantness. We work through the subtle machinations of phobic behavior in addition to working through the blocks, inhibitions and other protective attitudes.

To work through imaginary pains and unpleasant emotions we need a fine balance of frustration and support. Once the patient feels the essence of the "here and now" and "I and thou," he begins to understand his phobic behavior.

At first the patient will do anything to keep his attention from his actual experiences. He will take flight into memory and expectation (past and future); into the flight of ideas (free associations); intellectualizations or "making a case" of right and wrong. Finally, he encounters the holes in his personality with an awareness of nothing (no-thing-ness), emptiness, void and the impasse.

At last the patient comes to realize the hallucinatory character of his suffering. He discovers that "he does not have to" torture himself. He acquires a greater tolerance for frustration and imaginary pain. At this point he begins to mature.

I define maturity as the transition from environmental support to self-support. In Gestalt therapy maturity is achieved by developing the individual's own potential through decreasing environmental support, increasing his frustration tolerance and by debunking his phony *playing* of infantile and adult roles.

Resistance is great because the patient has been conditioned to manipulate his environment for support. He does this by acting helpless and stupid; he wheedles, bribes and flatters. He is *not infantile* but *plays an infantile* and dependent role expecting to control the situation by submissive behavior. He also plays the roles of an infantile adult. It is difficult for him to realize the difference between mature behavior and "playing an adult." With maturation the patient is increasingly able to mobilize spontaneously his own resources in order to deal with the environment. He learns to stand

From Planned Psychotherapy to Gestalt Therapy

on his own feet, thus becoming able to cope with his own problems as well as the exigencies of life.

Human potential is decreased both by inappropriate demands of society and by the inner conflict. Freud's parable of the two servants quarreling, with the resultant inefficiency, is again, in my opinion, but a half-truth. Actually, it is the masters who quarrel. In this case the opposing masters are what Freud named *superego* and *id*. The *id* in Freud's concept is a conglomeration of instincts and repressed memories. In actuality we observe in each and every case that the *superego* is opposed by a personalized entity which might be called *infraego*. In my language I call the opposing masters top dog and underdog. The struggle between the two is both internal and external.

Top-dog can be described as righteous, bullying, punishing, authoritarian and primitive. Top-dog commands continually with such statements as, "You should," "You ought to" and "Why don't you?" Oddly enough, we all so strongly identify with our inner top-dog that we no longer question its authority. We take its righteousness for granted.

Underdog develops great skill in evading top-dog's commands. Only half-heartedly intending to comply with the demands, underdog answers: "Yes, but . . . ," "I try so hard but next time I'll do better," and "Manana." Underdog usually gets the better of the conflict.

In other words, top- and underdog are actually two clowns performing their weird and unnecessary plays on the stage of the tolerant and mute self. Integration, or cure, can be achieved only when the need for mutual control between top- and underdogs ceases. Only then will the two masters mutually listen. Once they come to their senses (in this case listening to each other) does the door to integration and unification open. The chance of making a whole person out of a split becomes a certainty. The impasse of the

From Planned Psychotherapy to Gestalt Therapy

status quo or the eternal conflict of the non ending therapy can be overcome.

A gestaltist integration technique is dream work. We do not play psychoanalytical interpretation games. I have the suspicion that the dream is neither a fulfilled wish nor a prophecy of the future. To me it is an existential message. It tells the patient what his situation in life is and especially how to change the nightmare of his existence into becoming aware of and taking his historical place in life. In a successful cure the neurotic awakens from his trance of delusions. In Zen Buddhism the moment is called the great awakening *(satori)*. During Gestalt therapy the patient experiences a number of lesser awakenings. In coming to his senses he frequently sees the world brightly and clearly.

In actual practice I let the patient act out all the details of his dream. As therapists we do not imagine we know more than the patient does himself. We assume each part of the dream is a projection. Each fragment of the dream, be it person, prop or mood, is a portion of the patient's *alienated* self. Parts of the self are made to encounter other parts. The primary encounter, of course, is between top-dog and underdog.

To illustrate the method of integrating top- and underdogs by working through a dream, I relate a case of a patient who impressed everybody with his psychotic eccentricities. During one of my group sessions he related a dream in which he saw a young man enter a library, throw books about, shout and scream. When the librarian, an elderly spinster, rebuked him, he reacted with continued erratic behavior. In desperation the librarian summoned the police.

I directed my patient to act out and experience the encounter between the boy (underdog) and the librarian and police (topdogs). In the beginning the confrontation was belligerent and uselessly consuming of time and energy. After participating in the

From Planned Psychotherapy to Gestalt Therapy

hostile encounter for two hours, the different parts of my patient were able to stop fighting and listen to each other. True listening is understanding. He came to recognize that by playing "crazy" he could outwit his top-dog, because the irresponsible person is not punished. Following this successful integration the patient no longer needed to act crazy in order to be spontaneous. As a result he is now a freer and more amenable person. When top-dog feeds underdog expectations of success, results, improvements and changes, underdog generally responds with pseudo-compliance or sabotage. The result is inefficiency and spite. If the underdog sincerely tries to comply, he has the choice between an obsessional neurosis, flight into illness or "nervous breakdown." *The road to Hell is paved with good intentions.*

Externally, top- and underdogs struggle for control as well. Husband and wife, therapist and patient, employer and employees play out roles of mutual manipulation. The basic philosophy of Gestalt therapy is that of nature — differentiation and integration. Differentiation by itself leads to polarities. As dualities these polarities will easily fight and paralyze one another. By integrating opposite traits we make the person whole again. For instance, weakness and bullying integrate as silent firmness.

Such a person will have the perspective to see the total situation *(a gestalt)* without losing the details. With this improved orientation he is in a better position to cope with the situation by *mobilizing his own resources.* He no longer reacts with fixed responses (character) and preconceived ideas. He doesn't cry for environmental support, because he can do for himself. He no longer lives motivated by fears of impending catastrophes. He can now assess reality by *experimenting with possibilities.* He will *give up* control-madness and let the *situation* dictate his actions.

The ability to resign, to let go of obsolete responses, of exhausted relationships and of tasks beyond one's potential is an essential part of the wisdom of living.

From Planned Psychotherapy to Gestalt Therapy

Group vs. Individual Therapy

Reprinted from Etc: A Review of General Semantics, *Vol. 34, No. 3,1967, pp. 306-312, by permission of the International Society for General Semantics.*

Marshall McLuhan has written a book in which he expands the notion: the medium is the message.

What is the message we receive from the medium of group therapy? Group therapy tells us, "I am more economical than individual therapy." Individual therapy counters, "Yes, but you are less efficient." "But," asks group therapy, "who says you are efficient?"

You will notice that on my private stage these two therapies immediately begin to fight, to get into a conflict.

For a while, I tried to solve this conflict in Gestalt therapy by asking my patients to have both individual and group therapy. Lately, however, I have eliminated individual sessions altogether, except for emergency cases. As a matter of fact, I have come to consider that all individual therapy is obsolete and should be replaced by workshops in Gestalt therapy. In my workshops, I now

From Planned Psychotherapy to Gestalt Therapy

integrate individual and group work. This is effective with a group, however, only if the therapist's encounter with an *individual patient within the group* is effective.

To understand the effectiveness of Gestalt therapy in workshops, we have, first, to consider another conflict: the dichotomy in present-day psychology between the *experiential* and the *behavioral* approaches. Then we can understand how Gestalt therapy integrates both branches of psychology.

The behaviorist is usually thought of primarily as a conditioner. If he were willing to disassociate himself from the activity of conditioning — from a compulsion to change behavior, essentially by the external means of chill and repetition — he could become an observer, a describer of ongoing processes. He would then learn that learning is discovering, that it is a matter of new experience. On the other hand, he has one advantage over the majority of clinical psychologists: he works in the here and now. He is reality-oriented, though in a rather mechanical way; and he is more observation-oriented than the clinician, who, for the most part, is guided by abstractions and computations. But the clinician has what the behaviorist omits — full concern with the phenomenon of awareness. Whether he calls it consciousness, sensitivity, or awareness does not matter at all.

Freud assumed that the mere transposition of unconscious memories into conscious ones would be sufficient for a cure. Existential psychiatry has a similar, though somewhat broader, outlook: to assimilate and to make available all those parts of the personality that have been alienated.

What can hinder the experientialist is this: though his focus is on experience, he turns easily away from the here and now of the behaviorist. Either he becomes concerned, like Freud, with the past and with causality, or he becomes concerned, like Adler, with intentions. The actual behavior of *both* the therapist and the patient is

From Planned Psychotherapy to Gestalt Therapy

usually explained away as "transference" and "counter-transference."

Interest in observable behavior developed early in psychotherapy. The hypnotist wanted not only to relieve the patient of his symptoms, but also to change objectionable habits into desirable ones. The Freudian school saw behavior patterns parallel with the three recognized erogenous zones: oral, anal, and genital. Reich's interest in character formation was largely centered on a person's *motoric* behavior. He tried to take a short cut, and so, like most therapists, he neglected to observe the details of voice and *verbal* behavior.

The gestalt school has investigated much of our sensoric behavior. Since our contact with the world is based upon sensory awareness, especially seeing, hearing, and touching, these means of external object-awareness play as great a part in Gestalt therapy as does the internal proprioceptive system of self-awareness. Since all sensing takes place in the here and now, Gestalt therapy is "present time" oriented, as is the behaviorist.

The sum of the types of overt motoric and verbal behavior — that which is easily observable and verifiable — we call character. We call the place where this behavior originates the mind. Even our secret verbal behavior is called thinking or intellect. But it is actually fantasy, or, as Freud has seen it, to play in life — the rehearsal stage on which we prepare for the roles we want.

The intellect — the whole of intelligence — we might liken to a computer. It is, however, a pallid substitute for the vivid immediacy of sensing and experiencing. The psychoanalyst and the so-called rational therapist, by playing interpretation and explanation games, only reinforce this deceptive dominance of the intellect and interfere with the emotional responses which are at the center of our personality. In the emotional desert of neurotic patients, we

From Planned Psychotherapy to Gestalt Therapy

seldom find any feelings other than boredom, self-pity, and depression.

In short, the clinical psychotherapist lacks full involvement with actuality, with the here and now, whereas the behaviorist denies the importance of awareness. In Gestalt therapy, we integrate the two sides of the coin by doing microscopic psychiatry, by investigating the awareness and avoidance of awareness of every detail of the patient's and the so-called therapist's behavior. This is the true integration of the two psychologies — not just eclectic, not a compromise. But it is most difficult to achieve this synthesis in the combination of group and individual therapy.

A neurotic may be defined as a person who is unable to assume the full identity and responsibility of mature behavior. He will do anything to keep himself in the state of immaturity, even to playing the role of an adult — that is, his infantile concept of what an adult is like. The neurotic cannot conceive of himself as a self-supportive person, able to mobilize his potential in order to cope with the world. He looks for environmental support through direction, help, explanations, and answers. He mobilizes not his own resources, but his *means of manipulating* the environment — helplessness, flattery, stupidity, and other more or less subtle controls — in order to get support.

The psychoanalyst can play right into the hands of the neurotic who resorts to such behavior by disregarding the essence of human relationships and by turning any relationship into an infantile one, such as father-figure, incest, superego dominance. The patient is not made responsible, but the unconscious, the Oedipus complex or what-you-will, receives the catharsis of cause and responsibility.

The basic behavior of a student of mine was wailing. His father was a professional wailer: a cantor. The student *was aware* that he was like his father in many respects and fought this attitude; but the insight was of no help to him, because it never clarified what the essence of his wailing was. The louder he wailed, the greater his disappointment that there was no result. He failed to realize that he and his father were barking up the wrong tree. There could be no answer, because nobody, no God, no magician, was there to help him. The father imitation is not the problem. The irrational behavior of both father and son is.

Freudianism barks up the wrong tree of cause and interpretations; psychology in general does it by mixing up mind and fantasy. Every patient barks up the wrong tree by expecting that he can achieve maturation through external sources — through being psychoanalyzed, reconditioned, hypnotized, or marathonized, or by taking psychedelic drugs. Maturation cannot be achieved *for him*; he has to go through the painful process of growing up by himself. A therapist can do nothing but provide him with the opportunity — by being available both as a catalyst and as a screen upon which he can project his neurosis.

The basic theory of Gestalt therapy is that maturation is a continuous growth process in which environmental support is transformed into self-support. In healthy development, the infant mobilizes and learns to use his own resources. A viable balance of support and frustration enables him to become independent, free to utilize his innate potential.

In contrast, a neurosis develops in an environment that does not facilitate this maturation process adequately. Development is, instead, perverted into a character formation, into a set of behavior patterns that are meant to control the environment by manipulation.

The child learns, often by copying some adult, to secure environmental support by playing helpless or stupid, by bullying, by flattering, by trying to be seductive, and so on and on. Thus any helpful and too supportive therapist or member of the group who

From Planned Psychotherapy to Gestalt Therapy

is sucked in by a patient's manipulations will only spoil that person more — by depriving him of the opportunity to discover his own strength, potential, and resources. The therapist's real tool here is skillful frustration.

At the core of each neurosis lies what the Russians call the *sick point*. Realizing that they can do nothing to cure it, they are satisfied to reorganize it and to sublimate their energies around this sick point. In Gestalt therapy, we call this sick point the *impasse*; and I have as yet seen no method other than Gestalt therapy capable of getting through it. Furthermore, I doubt if it is possible to get through the impasse in individual therapy, and I know that the integration of individual and group therapy holds the possibility to do so.

When approaching the existential impasse (and this does not mean minor hang-ups), the patient gets into A whirl. He becomes panic-stricken, deaf and dumb — unwilling to leave the merry-go-round of compulsive repetition. He truly feels the despair which Kierkegaard recognized as "sickness unto death." The existential impasse is a situation in which no environmental support is forthcoming, and the patient is, or believes himself to be, incapable of coping with life on his own. So he will do anything to hold on to the status quo — rather than grow up and use his own powers. He will change marriage partners, but not his expectations; he will change therapists, but not his neurosis; he will change the content of his inner conflicts, but he will not give up his self-torture games; he will increase the subtlety of his manipulations and his control-madness to secure the environmental support without which he imagines he cannot survive.

Now, in the group situation something happens that is not possible in the private interview. To the whole group it is obvious that the person in distress does not see the obvious, does not see the way out of the impasse, does not see (for instance) that most of

From Planned Psychotherapy to Gestalt Therapy

his misery is a purely imagined one. In the face of this collective conviction of the group, he cannot use his usual phobic way of disowning the therapist when he cannot manipulate him. Somehow, trust in the group seems to be greater than trust in the therapist — in spite of all so-called transference confidence. Behind the impasse there lurks the threatening monster that keeps the patient nailed to the cross of his neurosis. This monster is the catastrophic expectation that, so he imagines, spells his doom and prevents him from taking reasonable risks and enduring the growing pains of maturation.

It is at this point that rational thinking has its place: in the assessment of the degree to which catastrophic expectation is mere imagination or exaggeration of real danger. In the safe emergency of the therapeutic situation, the neurotic discovers that the world does not fall to pieces if he gets angry, sexy, joyous, mournful. Nor is the group's support for his self-esteem and appreciation of his achievements toward authenticity and greater liveliness to be underestimated.

In my gestalt workshop anyone who feels the urge can work with me. I am available, but never pushing. A dyad is temporarily developed between myself and the patient; but the rest of the group is fully involved, though seldom as active participants. Mostly they act as an audience which is stimulated by the encounter to do quite a bit of silent self-therapy.

There are other advantages in working with a group. A great deal of individual development can be facilitated through doing collective experiments — talking gibberish together, or doing withdrawal experiments, or learning to understand the importance of atmosphere, or showing the person on the spot how he collectively bores, hypnotizes, or amuses the environment. In grief or similar emotionally charged situations, chain reactions often occur. The group soon learns to understand the contrast between helpfulness,

From Planned Psychotherapy to Gestalt Therapy

however well-meaning, and true support. And at the same time, the group's observation of the manipulative games which the neurotic plays, the roles he acts out in order to keep himself in the infantile state, facilitates their own self-recognition.

In other words, in contrast to the usual type of group meetings, I carry the load of the session, by either doing individual therapy or conducting mass experiments. I often interfere if the group plays opinion and interpretation games or has similar purely verbal encounters without any experiential substance, but I keep out of it as soon as anything genuine happens.

It is always a deeply moving experience for the group and for me, the therapist, to see previously robotized corpses begin to return to life, gain substance, begin the dance of abandonment and self-fulfillment. The *paper people are turning into real people.*

From Planned Psychotherapy to Gestalt Therapy

www.ingramcontent.com/pod-product-compliance
Lightning Source LLC
Chambersburg PA
CBHW020611270326
41927CB00005B/279

9 780939 266906